SAC ... ₹Y

D0485389

09

STERLING

CLEOPATRA

Egypt's Last and Greatest Queen

Susan Blackaby

STERLING

New York / London
www.sterlingpublishing.com/kids

For Emily and Chris, with thanks

STERLING and the distinctive Sterling logo are registered trademarks of
Sterling Publishing Co., Inc.

Library of Congress Cataloging-in-Publication Data
Blackaby, Susan.
  Cleopatra : Egypt's last and greatest queen / by Susan Blackaby.
    p. cm. — (Sterling biographies)
  Includes bibliographical references and index.
    ISBN 978-1-4027-5710-5 (pbk.) — ISBN 978-1-4027-6540-7 (hardcover)
  1. Cleopatra, Queen of Egypt, d. 30 B.C.—Juvenile literature. 2. Egypt—History—
332-30 B.C.—Juvenile literature. 3. Queens—Egypt—Biography—Juvenile literature.
I. Title.
  DT92.7.B58 2009
  932'.021092—dc22
  [B]
                              2008030146

10 9 8 7 6 5 4 3 2 1

Published by Sterling Publishing Co., Inc.
387 Park Avenue South, New York, NY 10016
© 2009 by Susan Blackaby
Distributed in Canada by Sterling Publishing
c/o Canadian Manda Group, 165 Dufferin Street
Toronto, Ontario, Canada M6K 3H6
Distributed in the United Kingdom by GMC Distribution Services
Castle Place, 166 High Street, Lewes, East Sussex, England BN7 1XU
Distributed in Australia by Capricorn Link (Australia) Pty. Ltd.
P.O. Box 704, Windsor, NSW 2756, Australia

Printed in China
All rights reserved

Sterling ISBN 978-1-4027-5710-5 (paperback)
          ISBN 978-1-4027-6540-7 (hardcover)

Image research by Larry Schwartz

For information about custom editions, special sales, premium and corporate
purchases, please contact Sterling Special Sales Department at 800-805-5489
or specialsales@sterlingpublishing.com.

Contents

INTRODUCTION: Playing to Win 1

CHAPTER 1: Birth of a Queen 2

CHAPTER 2: Power and Exile 11

CHAPTER 3: Appealing to Caesar 19

CHAPTER 4: Fighting for Control 25

CHAPTER 5: Devotion and Disaster 32

CHAPTER 6: Growing Conspiracies 42

CHAPTER 7: Passion and Politics 48

CHAPTER 8: Carefree and Careless 55

CHAPTER 9: Republican Unrest 61

CHAPTER 10: Reunion and Renewal 67

CHAPTER 11: The Parthian Campaign 75

CHAPTER 12: Triumphs, Titles, and Tensions 82

CHAPTER 13: Gathering Forces 90

CHAPTER 14: The Battle of Actium 98

CHAPTER 15: Death in Alexandria 109

GLOSSARY 118

BIBLIOGRAPHY 119

SOURCE NOTES 120

IMAGE CREDITS 122

ABOUT THE AUTHOR 122

INDEX 123

Events in the Life of Cleopatra

69 BCE

Winter 69 BCE
Cleopatra VII is born in Alexandria to Ptolemy XII and Cleopatra V. Cleopatra VI and Berenice are her older sisters; Arsinoë is her younger sister and is born about three years later.

61 BCE
Cleopatra's brother Ptolemy XIII is born.

59 BCE
Cleopatra's youngest brother, Ptolemy XIV, is born.

58 BCE
Ptolemy XII is forced to flee Alexandria. Cleopatra VI and Berenice seize control, but Cleopatra VI dies.

Spring 55 BCE
Ptolemy XII is restored to power; Berenice dies.

51 BCE
Ptolemy XII dies. Cleopatra VII and her brother-husband Ptolemy XIII are named co-regents. Cleopatra travels on the Nile to install the Buchis bull.

49 BCE
Cleopatra is forced into exile.

48 BCE
Julius Caesar arrives in Egypt; his rival, Pompey, is murdered. Cleopatra returns to Alexandria. The Alexandrian War begins.

Spring 47 BCE
Ptolemy XIII dies in battle, and the Alexandrian War ends. Caesar names Cleopatra and her brother-husband, Ptolemy XIV, co-regents. Cleopatra and Caesar travel on the Nile.

June 23, 47 BCE
Cleopatra gives birth to her first son, Ptolemy XV Caesar, who is called Caesarion.

September 46 BCE
Caesar's triumph is held in Rome; Cleopatra, Ptolemy XIV, and Caesarion join him there.

44 BCE
Caesar is murdered at the Senate in Rome on March 15. Cleopatra, Ptolemy XIV, and Caesarion return to Alexandria. Ptolemy XIV dies, and Caesarion is named co-regent.

41 BCE
Mark Antony and Cleopatra meet in Tarsus and spend the winter in Alexandria.

October 40 BCE
Mark Antony marries Octavia in Rome. Cleopatra gives birth to twins, Alexander Helios and Cleopatra Selene.

Fall 37 BCE
Mark Antony and Cleopatra are reunited and spend the winter of 37–36 in Antioch.

Fall 36 BCE
Cleopatra gives birth to Ptolemy Philadelphus. Mark Antony launches the Parthian campaign and is defeated.

32 BCE
Mark Antony divorces Octavia. Octavian declares war on Cleopatra on behalf of Rome.

September 2, 31 BCE
Octavian defeats Cleopatra and Mark Antony at the Battle of Actium. Mark Antony deserts his troops to follow Cleopatra to Alexandria.

Spring 30 BCE
Octavian attacks Egypt.

August 1, 30 BCE
Mark Antony is defeated by Octavian. Mark Antony commits suicide.

August 12, 30 BCE
Cleopatra dies. The Ptolemaic dynasty, founded in 305 BCE, comes to an end.

30 BCE

Playing to Win

Whatever Cleopatra dictated was done, without regard for the laws of man or nature.

—Appian

According to legend, Mark Antony hosted a magnificent feast for Cleopatra and waited for praise from Egypt's powerful queen. After all, had the Roman general not met her superior standards of luxury and extravagance? In the candlelight, Cleopatra's jewels sparkled. Her dark eyes flashed. Mark Antony may have spared no expense, but Cleopatra could not be outdone. She dismissed his efforts, saying that she could spend an amount equal to 60,000 pounds of gold on a single meal. Mark Antony challenged her to prove it.

The next night Cleopatra hosted a superb banquet, but Mark Antony must have felt confident. Nothing gracing the table or passing their lips came close to meeting her impressive claim. However, the meal was not yet finished.

Cleopatra's servant brought her a goblet of vinegar. The queen removed an earring. The pearl dangling from the gold clasp—one of the two largest pearls in the world—was worth an astronomical sum. Cleopatra dropped the earring into the drink and swirled it until the pearl dissolved. Without hesitation, she drank the mixture and then flashed Mark Antony a victorious smile.

At that moment, Mark Antony learned a valuable lesson.

Cleopatra—daring, clever, smart, rich, determined, and rash—intended to win at any cost.

CHAPTER 1

Birth of a Queen

Egypt has three hundred cities, plus three thousand, plus three times ten thousand, plus two times three, plus three times nine, and king Ptolemy rules them all.

—Theocritus

In the winter of 69 **BCE**, Egypt's ruler welcomed a third baby girl into the royal family. King Ptolemy XII named his daughter Cleopatra, which in Greek means "her father's glory." She joined a **dynasty** that had ruled Egypt for more than 250 years.

The Ptolemy Family

The Ptolemy family came originally from Macedonia, a kingdom located in the northern region of ancient Greece. They rose to power after the death of Alexander the Great, a brilliant military leader who had established an **empire** that extended eastward from Greece to India. He conquered Egypt in

This seventeenth-century copper medallion shows Cleopatra's father, Ptolemy Auletes, holding Poseidon's trident and wearing Helios's crown—symbols that link him to Greek gods.

331 BCE and mapped out the plan for a new capital city that would bear his name. When Alexander died in 323 BCE, his close circle of advisers divided the empire into three regions—Macedon, Syria, and Egypt. In the division, Alexander's trusted general and childhood friend, Ptolemy, claimed Egypt for himself. He knew about Alexander's dream to build the most remarkable city in the world and saw to it that this dream was fulfilled.

The kingdoms that had been part of Alexander's empire maintained strong cultural ties to Greece. However, from the beginning of their reign, the Ptolemies combined their Greek heritage with Egyptian customs that could be traced back thousands of years. King Ptolemy I called himself the pharaoh, in keeping with the Egyptian kings and queens who ruled before him.

Using the Egyptian title of pharaoh linked Ptolemy to Egyptian history and to the power of the Egyptian gods. Nevertheless, Ptolemy did not entirely give up his Greek ways. He still dressed in the woolen robes that citizens of Athens wore. He spoke Greek. He worshipped the Greek gods. Ptolemy passed this legacy down through the ages. Generations later, Cleopatra inherited the **Ptolemaic** traits and traditions. She was an Egyptian citizen, but Greek blood flowed in her veins.

Cleopatra's father, Ptolemy XII, was called Auletes, which means "the flute player." He was known far and wide for hosting huge parties and fancy banquets. The identity of her mother is uncertain, but it is likely that she was Ptolemy XII's sister, Cleopatra V. The pharaohs had long practiced brother-sister marriage. In doing so, they copied the lives of the gods and goddesses they worshipped. The Greek myths favored by the Ptolemies featured similar relationships. For example, the Greek god Zeus was

She was an Egyptian citizen, but Greek blood flowed in her veins.

Rulers and Gods

The word *pharaoh* comes from the Egyptian phrase *per-ao*, meaning "great house." Over time, it came to refer to the king or queen living in the great house, a divine ruler who was considered a god.

In Egypt, government and religion were two parts of a whole. The strength of Egypt as a nation and its endurance as a society can be traced to the key role the pharaoh played as a direct link to the gods. In dynasty after dynasty, the people may have objected to the policies of one ruler or another. Nevertheless, the pharaoh commanded great respect and support due to his or her close relationship to the gods.

This mural, created c. 1200–1085 BCE, depicts the pharaoh, Ramses III, and his son making offerings in the underworld to Apis, the sacred bull that stood for the god Osiris.

married to his sister, Hera. Together they ruled over the rest of the Greek gods and goddesses. It is therefore not so surprising that the Ptolemies chose to continue this ancient marriage custom between members of the Egyptian royal family.

Cleopatra—historically known as Cleopatra VII—grew up with five sisters and brothers at the palace in Alexandria. Two sisters—Cleopatra VI and Berenice—were older. Another sister, Arsinoë, was born about three years after Cleopatra. Later came two boys. Ptolemy XIII was born in 61 BCE, and Ptolemy XIV was born in 59 BCE. All of the children were raised to carry on the dynasty. According to the Egyptian law that the Ptolemies followed, women were allowed to take the throne and rule in their own right or as equal partners alongside the men. Cleopatra and her sisters received the same education as their brothers to prepare them for the responsibilities of ruling an empire.

Alexandria

When Alexander laid out the grid for the port city of Alexandria, the site he chose was a quiet coastal village west of the Nile Delta. By the time Cleopatra was born, Alexandria had become the largest and grandest city in the world. Its population had grown to 300,000 citizens made up of different groups. The powerful Greek community, which was the ruling class, lived in the center of the city. The Jewish community, mostly scholars and tradesmen, lived on the east side. The Egyptians, who were considered second-class citizens, lived in the old part of the city

Alexandria's lively elegance is shown in this illustration of the waterfront.

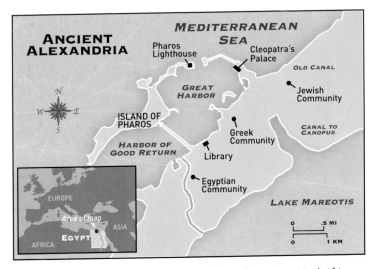

Alexandria's location made it a lively trade center for goods coming to North Africa from Rome and goods carried over the Silk Road from Asia.

on the west side. Cleopatra herself lived in the royal district called the Bruchion, a cluster of palaces overlooking the Mediterranean Sea on the northeast side of the city.

The city proper swarmed with people from all walks of life. Merchants, sailors, artisans, government workers, and soldiers lived crowded together. Even so, city life was comfortable and pleasant, thanks to the wide streets, parks, gardens, and extensive system of canals. The river and nearby Lake Mareotis, located south of the city, provided a steady supply of fresh water; and sea breezes kept the air circulating.

The location of Alexandria on the Mediterranean made it a major trade center. Two harbors flanked a causeway connecting the island of Pharos to the mainland. The causeway extended for about three-quarters of a mile. The magnificent Pharos lighthouse guided ships into the Great Harbor on the east side

The Pharos Lighthouse

The Pharos lighthouse was one of the Seven Wonders of the ancient world. The marble structure was ordered by Ptolemy I and designed by Sostrates in 290 BCE. Built in three sections, it had a square base and an octagonal midsection. A giant statue of Zeus stood on the round chamber at the top. The tower rose to an overall height of 423 feet, making it the tallest building in the world at that time. While the other world wonders were purely decorative or ceremonial, the lighthouse was used to guide ships into port. In the top chamber, a huge curved mirror made of polished bronze reflected sunlight during the day. At night, it reflected light from a burning flame. The beacon could be seen from more than thirty miles out at sea.

Artists use historic descriptions to imagine what the Pharos lighthouse looked like. Johann Bernhard Fischer von Eriach created this etching in 1721.

of the causeway and the Harbor of Good Return on the west. Each harbor was big enough to hold 1,200 vessels at one time. Goods from Africa, Asia, Greece, and Italy arrived by sea and by overland routes. The historian named Strabo declared the marketplace in Alexandria to be "the greatest emporium in the inhabited world." Cleopatra would have been exposed to all sorts of tastes and treasures sold in the shops and stalls lining the streets.

This illustration shows scholars studying papyrus scrolls stored in the library that Cleopatra used in Alexandria.

Besides being a trading hub, Alexandria also had a long history as a center for culture and learning. Great thinkers, teachers, writers, dramatists, and artists shaped its colorful past. Ptolemy I founded the Museum, which became a center for scientific study. Ptolemy II established the Library and vowed to collect one copy of every manuscript in existence. Thanks to these **patrons**, Cleopatra had access to an enormous body of knowledge for reading and research.

Learning to Rule

The details of Cleopatra's childhood are unknown, but there is no doubt that she was extremely well educated. The pharaohs of Egypt had a long-standing program to educate their daughters to prepare them to rule, and this was one of the traditions that the Ptolemies followed, too. They even extended education for girls to the daughters of wealthy Greeks who were part of the ruling class. Schools set up across Egypt trained the leaders and administrators of the future.

Records show that Cleopatra studied subjects based on Greek literature. Greek works considered the masterpieces of the day were collected into a set of textbooks for her. Cleopatra read Homer's epics, *The Iliad* and *The Odyssey*; poetry by Hesiod and

Pindar; and plays by Euripides and Menander. She studied history written by Herodotus and Thucydides, which included **political** and military events of the past, and memorized the speeches of Demosthenes to learn the fine points of public speaking and debate.

Records show that Cleopatra studied subjects based on Greek literature.

In addition to literature, Cleopatra studied science and math. Subjects included arithmetic, geometry, astronomy, and medicine. To round out her education, Cleopatra studied art and music, and for recreation, she sailed and rode horses. In every aspect, her education prepared her morally, mentally, and physically to step into her role as queen.

Cleopatra seems to have been a curious and eager student. While it is certain that she was extremely bright, she was truly exceptional when it came to learning foreign languages. Reports that she knew as many as nine languages fluently and could move from one to another without effort may be exaggerated. Nevertheless, it is true that she was the only Ptolemy ever to learn to speak Egyptian, and she was one of the few members of her family able to converse with neighboring dignitaries in their own tongue. Her language skills made her useful in political discussions. It also earned her the respect and affection of the Egyptian people living outside the Greek influence of Alexandria.

Support from Rome

Although Egypt was isolated by the surrounding desert and maintained its political independence, the Ptolemies had come to rely on the vast power of the Roman **Republic** to provide support and to help keep order. The Ptolemies paid Rome to protect them from uprisings by native Egyptians and occasional threats from

The Roman Republic

In the centuries after Alexander's death, marking the end of his empire, Rome rose to the level of a superpower. Roman generals used military might to extend their territory. In some cases the generals shared leadership of the annexed territories with local officials. In other cases they put Roman governors and representatives in place to rule newly acquired regions. Everyone answered to the Senate in Rome. By the time Cleopatra was born, the Roman Republic stretched across Europe, extended east to the Euphrates River, and included parts of North Africa.

tribes to the east. Cleopatra's father continued this policy, making sure that Egypt stayed on Rome's good side at any cost.

Ptolemy XII could be weak, harsh, and unpredictable. He thought nothing of bankrupting his own people to buy Rome's protection. At the same time, he did anything he could to strengthen his own authority and granted favors to anyone who would assist in this effort. Cleopatra saw for herself the power plays, secret pacts, broken promises, **bribes**, and betrayals that marked her father's rule.

On the other hand, Cleopatra could look all around her and see the glories of the Ptolemaic dynasty as well. Marble monuments graced the wide streets of Alexandria. Gilded temples, restored to their former grandeur, gleamed in the desert sun. Murals depicted her ancestors as powerful god-rulers who presided over a rich land. The tombs of the pharaohs and of Alexander the Great himself served as constant reminders of the heights she could hope to achieve.

CHAPTER 2

Power and Exile

*The Queen, the Lady of the Two Lands, the goddess
who loves her father . . .*
—*The Buchis Stela*

By 58 BCE, Ptolemy's subjects were paying huge sums to
buy Rome's protection. The Alexandrians, who resented
Rome's increasing claims of authority over them, began to
speak out. As unrest grew, Ptolemy's only choice was to
seek Rome's help, further angering the citizens.

Julius Caesar and Pompey, two of the three generals
who shared the ruling power in Rome, agreed to provide
Ptolemy with the support he needed, but it came at a very
high price. Ptolemy borrowed a huge sum of money to
meet their demands, stacking debt upon debt for his
subjects to repay. Adding to the crisis, he stood by and let
Rome take control of the Egyptian island of Cyprus. The
Romans had already threatened Egyptian borders by seizing
control of neighboring Syria. Now the Roman army seemed
to be getting ready for a complete takeover.

Fearing for their independence, the Alexandrians
launched a revolt against the pharaoh. King Ptolemy fled
the city and made his way to Rome. In his absence, his
eldest daughters, Cleopatra VI and Berenice, took charge.

Family Betrayals

Instead of acting on Ptolemy's behalf, Berenice soon
got rid of Cleopatra VI and seized complete control of her

father's reign. Some reports suggest that Berenice had Cleopatra VI poisoned. Records from the time simply state that Berenice and her second husband, Archilaus, ruled jointly after Berenice had her first husband strangled. It is also unclear whether the younger Cleopatra went into exile with her father. She may have stayed in Alexandria with her sisters. In any event, Cleopatra knew about Berenice's murdering ways, and she understood that people would do anything to achieve and maintain power.

Once he arrived safely in Rome, Ptolemy went to work lobbying for support. He borrowed more money to bribe senators who could help him reclaim his throne. When delegates arrived from Alexandria to argue against restoring his power, Ptolemy had them murdered. He offered Gabinius—the Roman governor of Syria, a kingdom under Rome's control—a huge sum for the loan of his army.

In the spring of 55 BCE, Gabinius's army marched on Alexandria. In the raid that followed, Berenice's husband, Archilaus, was killed. The Alexandrians, who were completely outmatched, quickly gave up the fight. Ptolemy returned to the capital as a conquering hero.

Restored to power, Ptolemy took steps to make sure that his position would be secure. First, he had his daughter Berenice executed for her treachery.

Gabinius played an important political role in Rome as one of Pompey's biggest supporters. This bust was found in Herculaneum, which was buried when Mt. Vesuvius erupted in 79 CE.

Second, he made his main moneylender from Rome a top adviser. The adviser heaped huge taxes on the Egyptians to ensure that Ptolemy's debts would be paid in full. (This was a clever move on Ptolemy's part. He knew that it would not take long for the angry Egyptians to run the tax collector out of the country—which is exactly what happened.) Third and most important, he drew up his will. He named fourteen-year-old Cleopatra and her six-year-old brother Ptolemy XIII as his successors to make it clear that the dynasty would continue. He then filed the document with the Roman Senate, putting the might of Rome behind his wishes in case the Egyptians had ideas about taking control. Pompey was appointed to serve as the children's guardian.

Portrait du Jeune Ptolomée dernier Roi d'Égypte tiré d'un Médaillon Antique d'argent

This antique silver medallion depicts Ptolemy XIII, Cleopatra's younger brother and co-ruler, who came to power at the age of ten.

Lady of the Two Lands

In 51 BCE, Ptolemy XII became ill and died. Following the laws of the dynasty, Cleopatra and her brother Ptolemy XIII married and took their place on the Egyptian throne. Cleopatra was eighteen years old. Ptolemy XIII was ten. The marriage was simply a matter of form, and Ptolemy XIII served as pharaoh in name only. Cleopatra had complete freedom to decide how best to rule the kingdom.

Her official title became Queen Cleopatra VII Philopator ("she who loves her father"), Lady of the Two Lands. It referred to her power over both Upper Egypt and Lower Egypt. It also referred to

This illustration uses veils, jewels, and a crown to show Queen Cleopatra's beauty and power. An Egyptian serpent bracelet is coiled around her arm.

her positive connection to Ptolemy XII. Her older sisters had scorned their father by seizing control after he was forced to flee Alexandria. Cleopatra wanted everyone to understand—and remember—that she had his blessing in claiming her place as pharaoh.

Cleopatra's title also showed the level of loyalty and affection she felt toward her father's memory. From Cleopatra's point of view, Ptolemy XII had been betrayed by his subjects, who sent him into exile and tried to have him overthrown. He had been manipulated by Rome, paying dearly for Egypt's independence. Cleopatra would not soon forget how her father had been treated.

Earning Respect in Egypt and Rome

Cleopatra had strong ties to her father, to her family's long history on the throne, and to her Greek heritage. She also felt a deep connection to the Egyptian people. She identified with the Egyptian goddess Isis, the partner of the god-king Osiris, who the Egyptians believed had ruled as pharaoh on Earth. She respected the Egyptian customs and rituals. Her participation in these ancient rites helped her to earn the approval and respect of her subjects.

Cleopatra identified with Isis, the Egyptian goddess of the throne who oversaw motherhood, marriage, and nature. Isis is shown here in a copy of a wall painting from c. 1360 BCE.

Only a short time after becoming queen, Cleopatra took part in the installation of the Buchis bull—one of the divine animals worshipped by the Egyptians. For a bull to be chosen as the Buchis bull, it had to be a specific color and have special markings on it, and when a Buchis bull died, priests gave it a sacred burial.

In order to bring the new Buchis bull to its temple at Hermonthis, a city near Thebes in Upper Egypt, Cleopatra traveled more than four hundred miles on the Nile by boat. The royal procession gave her a chance to honor an ancient rite, which helped her win over the priests and landholders. It also gave her a chance to connect with her subjects. Cleopatra relied on her commanding presence to show her people the strength and power she would bring to her reign.

This sandstone slab was made between 284 and 246 BCE. It shows King Ptolemy II offering bread to the Buchis bull so that it will be well fed throughout eternity.

Ruling Alone

In the inscription that describes Cleopatra's participation in the ceremony of the Buchis bull, no mention is made of Ptolemy XIII. It is likely that Cleopatra was at this point ruling independently because Ptolemy was so young.

At around the same time, records show that Cleopatra also acted alone when she arrested Roman soldiers responsible for murdering the sons of the new Roman governor of Syria. The soldiers had stayed on in Alexandria after restoring Ptolemy XII to power. Life for these Roman soldiers was relaxing and carefree compared to what they might be required to do elsewhere. The governor sent his sons to order the men back to active duty, but the soldiers refused to go. In the scuffle that followed, the governor's sons were killed. Cleopatra upheld the laws of Rome and sent the accused men back to Italy to stand trial. Doing so showed that her father's ties to Rome extended to her reign as well. It also gave her a chance to demonstrate her cooperation and loyalty, hoping to get the same in return.

The Nile River

The Sahara desert covers the northern part of the African continent, stretching from the Atlantic Ocean to the Red Sea. The Nile River, flowing slowly through a shallow valley, is the only thing that interrupts thousands of miles of empty sand. A thin ribbon of lush vegetation traces its banks where it crosses the barren landscape. The Nile is Egypt's lifeline.

During the rainy season from July to October, heavy rains fall in the central African highlands. Water cascades over cliffs and crags. It pools in lakes and swirls through canyons. Streams fill and merge to join the Nile River system that drains into the Mediterranean Sea more than 4,000 miles to the north.

This c. 1950 photograph shows the floodplains of the Nile. For centuries, Egyptians depended on the heavy rainfall and annual flooding that provided rich topsoil and irrigation to the otherwise stark landscape.

In Cleopatra's day, six cataracts, or waterfalls, carried surging floodwater into Egypt where it overflowed the banks of the Nile and spread out across the plain. When the floodwater receded, it left behind a layer of fertile, black soil. Egyptian farmers raised a wide variety of fruits and vegetables—harvesting rich vineyards, tending extensive orchards, and producing record amounts of grain for domestic use and for export.

Sibling Treachery

Closer to home, Cleopatra needed to be on guard for ruthless enemies within her own family. After all, she came from a long line of backstabbing, power-hungry rivals. Many of them would stop at nothing to achieve their goals. Arsinoë, for one, might gladly unseat her older sister given half the chance. Although the boy-husband-king Ptolemy XIII did not pose much of a threat to Cleopatra on his own, his advisers—Pothinus, Achillas, and Theodotus—most certainly did. Pothinus was Ptolemy's servant, Achillas was his general, and Theodotus was his tutor. Little by little, they had gained complete control over the young king. Conspiring against Cleopatra kept them very busy indeed, and their efforts would soon be rewarded.

Closer to home, Cleopatra needed to be on guard for ruthless enemies within her own family.

At the beginning of 49 BCE, **papyrus** documents and decrees listed Ptolemy XIII and Cleopatra as joint rulers. In March of that year, the phrase "King Ptolemy and Queen Cleopatra, the gods who love their father" appeared on two separate contracts. These sketchy records show that Cleopatra was not only ruling alongside her brother, but also that she was now second in command. While it is impossible to know exactly what was happening, it is clear that power was shifting within the palace at Alexandria. In October, the Roman Senate declared Ptolemy to be "a friend and **ally**" of Rome. Cleopatra's name was nowhere to be found. Ptolemy's powerful advisers had forced her into exile.

Cleopatra fled across the Arabian Desert to Syria and set about raising an army. In the summer of 48 BCE, she was ready to confront her brother and reclaim her place on the throne.

CHAPTER 3

Appealing to Caesar

Interaction with her was captivating . . .
      —Plutarch

Prepared to put up a fight to prevent Cleopatra's return to power, thirteen-year-old Ptolemy assembled the royal army near Pelusium—a fortress city on the eastern bank of the Nile. Cleopatra knew that getting past Ptolemy's army would be difficult, if not impossible. Pelusium had protected Egypt from invasion for thousands of years, and from there it was a six-day march to Alexandria. Cleopatra had brains and outrage and will on her side, but her success would also require a lot of luck.

For Cleopatra, luck came in the form of the **civil** war being waged between Caesar and Pompey, the two generals who now ruled Rome.

Caesar and Pompey

The conflict between Julius Caesar and Pompey had been going on for more than a year as the two generals fought for supreme power over the Roman Republic. After badly beating Pompey on the battlefield in northern

Pompey the Great (106 BCE–48 BCE) rose to great power as one of Rome's rulers. This nineteenth-century wood engraving depicts him fleeing after his loss to Julius Caesar at Pharsalus in 48 BCE.

Greece, Caesar chased Pompey's fleet to Egypt. When Pompey arrived at Pelusium ahead of Caesar, he found King Ptolemy camped with his army, waiting for Cleopatra.

Pompey asked to meet with the king to remind him of their long-standing family and political ties and to request a safe harbor and support. Pompey had every reason to expect a certain amount of help and loyalty from Egypt. After all, he had gotten Ptolemy XII restored to his place on the throne, and he held a trusted position with the family as young Ptolemy's guardian. The king owed Pompey plenty of favors, and Pompey intended to collect.

However, Ptolemy's advisers Pothinus, Achillas, and Theodotus intercepted Pompey's request. They argued about what to do. How should Pompey be handled? If they helped Pompey, Caesar might become angry. After all, Caesar's latest victory made it clear that he had the upper hand, and it would not be in Egypt's best interests to side with Caesar's enemy. They further reasoned that sending Pompey away could anger both Romans. Pompey would resent being ignored, and Caesar might blame Egypt for dragging out their conflict. Besides that, they did not want Caesar and Pompey's next battle to be waged on Egyptian soil. Thanks to the power struggle between Ptolemy and Cleopatra, **resources** and supplies were already running low. Egypt could not afford to support another war.

The king owed Pompey plenty of favors, and Pompey intended to collect.

After much debate, Theodotus convinced the other advisers that the only clear choice was to kill Pompey. With Pompey out of the way, they would not have to worry about his demands. At the same time, they would win Caesar's favor and gratitude for taking care of his rival once and for all. They sent a boat to fetch Pompey to the shore. Pompey, uneasy about the meeting, bid farewell

Caesar reacts with dismay, disbelief, and disgust when Theodotus presents him with Pompey's head, as shown in this etching from 1820.

to his wife with Sophocles's quote: "Whoever has dealings with a tyrant is his slave, even if he goes as a free man." As soon as Pompey boarded the boat, the army escort stabbed him to death.

Pothinus put Pompey's severed head in a basket and arranged to have it delivered to Caesar, who had sailed to Alexandria. Ptolemy's advisers thought that the gruesome trophy would please Caesar and would send him on his way.

It did not. On the contrary, Pompey's death came as a shock. Caesar may have been glad to discover that he had at last become the most powerful man in Rome. Nevertheless, he was a soldier, and he valued a fair fight. Pompey's murder was the work of cowards. Besides that, Pompey had been married to Caesar's daughter. The two men had a long history of mutual respect and friendship in spite of their political struggles. Caesar insisted on a proper burial for his fallen opponent.

Caesar in Alexandria

Julius Caesar marched into Alexandria and set up camp in the palace. He needed to settle the dispute between Ptolemy and Cleopatra so that he could tap into their resources. Pompey was gone, but Pompey's men were still going strong. Caesar needed money to finance his campaign against them.

When Pothinus found out that Caesar was not leaving Alexandria, he rushed Ptolemy back from Pelusium. As instructed,

Julius Caesar (100 BCE–44 BCE)

Julius Caesar was born in July of 100 BCE. He belonged to the Julian clan, which traced its roots back to Rome's founders. He was known for his elegance in speech, his exacting habits, and his eloquent writing. As the historian and biographer Suetonius described him, "He is said to have been tall in stature and fair in complexion, to have had shapely limbs, a somewhat large mouth, dark and lively eyes, and good health . . ." Caesar's military genius helped the Romans conquer Spain and Gaul (modern-day France and Belgium), and he worked his way up through the political ranks to challenge Pompey for control of the Republic.

Andrea Andreani created this woodcut, titled *The Triumph of Julius Caesar*, in 1598 or 1599. It shows a procession to honor the victorious general.

Ptolemy did his best to make his guest feel unwelcome. The "feast" presented to Caesar and his troops consisted of spoiled grain served on chipped pottery. Ptolemy and his advisers did not want Caesar to get the idea that Egypt had any wealth to spare. In fact, their actions were meant to imply that Caesar had already looted the palace and stolen all the silver.

Meanwhile, Cleopatra was hatching a plan to get the power of Rome behind her. She knew that Caesar might be her only hope to regain her rightful place on Egypt's throne. She needed to meet with him face to face, but Ptolemy's army blocked her path to Alexandria. Even if she could get past the troops at Pelusium, Ptolemy's advisers would have her killed the minute she set foot inside the city. She had to find another way.

Cleopatra put her future in the hands of her trusted friend, Apollodorus. The two of them traveled by boat along the coast. Near sundown, they managed to sneak into the harbor at Alexandria. Once they docked, Cleopatra had Apollodorus roll her up in a carpet. Apollodorus tied the bundle with a leather strap. He then carried it up through the city and easily slipped past the palace guards. He delivered it to Caesar in his private chambers.

Caesar unrolled the carpet and discovered the queen.

In *Cleopatra Before Caesar*, Jean Léon Gérôme captures Caesar's surprise as Apollodorus unrolls the carpet to reveal the young queen. Gérôme's oil painting dates from 1866.

Love at First Sight

Enchanted by her clever and daring trick, Caesar fell in love with Cleopatra at first sight. The historian Plutarch wrote that "interaction with [Cleopatra] was captivating, and her appearance, along with her persuasiveness in discussion and her character that accompanied all interaction, was stimulating." Her magnetic charm stemmed from her quick wit and keen intellect. It is no wonder that Caesar and Cleopatra were drawn to each other. Her brilliance was matched only by his power. Together they made an impressive couple.

Early the next morning, Caesar asked to meet with Ptolemy, who was furious to find Cleopatra safe inside the palace, winning over the most powerful man in the world. In a rage, he ran outside. He threw off his crown. He shouted to the crowd that he had been double-crossed. Caesar ordered his soldiers to take Ptolemy into custody. Then he addressed the crowd with both Ptolemy and Cleopatra at his side. He declared that the two would rule Egypt together, as their father's will decreed. Rome would supervise them. In a show of goodwill, he gave the island of Cyprus back to Egypt. He put Cleopatra's younger siblings, Arsinoë and Ptolemy XIV, in charge of it so that everyone would be happy.

Everyone was not happy.

Cleopatra's Charm

In the blur of history, Cleopatra's political power is linked to her breathtaking beauty. Artwork, plays, and films portray her as being both glamorous and gorgeous. In fact, existing likenesses and ancient texts reveal that she was not especially attractive. She apparently inherited her father's large hooked nose and could, at best, be called pleasant if ordinary looking. However, by all accounts she was irresistible.

This etching from the 1800s shows Cleopatra with features that match those of her father. Her crown, jewels, and clothing combine Greek and Egyptian symbols.

CHAPTER 4

Fighting for Control

Caesar handed over the kingdom to the young boy and the elder of the two daughters, Cleopatra, who continued to enjoy his loyalty and protection.

— *Julius Caesar*

Ptolemy's advisers knew that if Cleopatra allied with Caesar, they stood to lose all their power. They needed to get rid of Caesar and send the Romans on their way. At the end of October, the royal army—still camped at Pelusium—marched on Alexandria, led by Ptolemy's general, Achillas. Achillas hoped that Caesar, with only a handful of troops to hold the city, would be forced to retreat. However, Caesar stood his ground. He set up headquarters in the palace to protect the royal family as the fighting flared around them. The battle, which came to be known as the Alexandrian War, lasted for four months.

Battle Tactics

Caesar's troops may have been vastly outnumbered, but Caesar fought back, using the daring and ruthless moves that made him famous. When the Alexandrians poisoned the royal water supply, Caesar had his men dig new wells. When the Alexandrians tried to take the harbor, Caesar set fire to their ships. When Pothinus—who was still acting as Ptolemy's adviser—made a secret pact with Achillas, Caesar punished this betrayal of the Ptolemies by having Pothinus executed.

Behind the scenes, Princess Arsinoë was making mischief of her own. With Caesar in command and Alexandria under siege, she assumed that Cleopatra and Ptolemy's power was hers for the taking. She escaped from the palace and joined forces with Achillas, declaring she was the queen. Arsinoë and Achillas soon became locked in a power struggle themselves, going behind each other's backs to bribe the troops and gain control. Following in her family's footsteps, Arsinoë had Achillas murdered by her supporters to clear her path to the throne.

Left without a commander, the Alexandrians asked Caesar to send Ptolemy to lead them. They promised that if the king told them to surrender, they would lay down their arms. Caesar advised Ptolemy to be faithful to the Romans and to consider the welfare of the Egyptian people. Ptolemy may have agreed to honor his duty to Rome. However, once he reached the battlefield, he willingly continued the fight.

Ptolemy was a headstrong boy, not a military mastermind. He took command just as Caesar's reinforcements finally arrived. Caesar led his troops in an ambush. The Romans sneaked up behind Ptolemy's encampment and pushed his army back to the banks of the Nile. In the final confrontation, Ptolemy drowned. With his death, the Alexandrian War came to an abrupt end.

On March 27, 47 BCE, Caesar marched through Alexandria and took his place beside Cleopatra. He carried

Julius Caesar is shown on his horse as a conquering hero, confident in his role as a leader and commanding respect from those whom he would control.

Ptolemy's golden armor as an emblem of his victory. The Alexandrians bowed down before him. They begged for mercy, which Caesar did not hesitate to grant. He still needed Egypt's wealth to finance his army. Caesar had long-range plans to increase the size and strength of the Roman Republic. It was in his best interests to establish a stable government in Egypt and a lasting peace with the queen and her people.

Giving Egypt Back to the Ptolemies

When the Alexandrian War ended in 47 BCE, Caesar's victory made him the conqueror. He had an opportunity to make Egypt part of the Republic. This may seem like a tempting move, but it had its down side. In order to **annex** Egypt, Caesar needed to install a representative to govern it. Anyone controlling Egypt gained access to its enormous treasury and unlimited resources. A Roman governor could raise a huge army and mobilize the extensive fleet. He could challenge Caesar's power and even launch a campaign to take over the entire Roman Republic. It was safer for Caesar to give Egypt back to the Ptolemies. He could keep Cleopatra in a position of needing to trade resources and money for protection and independence. That way, he took advantage of Egypt's wealth without having to worry about a rival.

It was Caesar's custom to reward those who had aided his cause. Except for Arsinoë, whom he imprisoned and sent to Rome, he did not punish his former enemies. To restore order, Caesar reread Ptolemy XII's will and vowed to carry out his wishes. According to the rules of the dynasty, Cleopatra now married her youngest brother, Ptolemy XIV, and resumed her seat on the throne as Egypt's pharaoh. Ptolemy XIV was about twelve years old. Cleopatra, now twenty-two, once again had the complete power she craved.

Here, Cleopatra is dressed in the Egyptian style. Illustrator Walter Paget (1863–1935) has depicted her wearing a headdress that features the cobra, a symbol of her rule over Lower Egypt.

Caesar appointed a guard made up of three **legions** (15,000–18,000 men) to stay in Alexandria. They were charged with keeping the peace; looking out for his interests; and watching over his lover, Cleopatra. The rest of Caesar's troops wanted to leave Egypt and turn their attention to other campaigns, but on Caesar's orders, they stayed . . . and stayed. Egypt and Cleopatra both fascinated Caesar. He was in no hurry to be on his way.

The Lovers' Voyage

In the spring of 47 BCE, Cleopatra and Caesar embarked on a cruise on the Nile. They traveled aboard the royal barge, tended by a fleet of 400 other vessels. From their luxurious accommodations, they could take in fabulous sights as they passed the ancient ruins and famous monuments of Egyptian culture, including the Pyramids and the Sphinx. No doubt, Caesar basked in the attention they received. After all, the Egyptians considered Cleopatra divine and treated her accordingly. Caesar was a powerful man and conquering hero of the Roman Republic, but at the end of the day, he was merely a public official. He was not a king, and he certainly was not a god.

Ancient Wonders

By the time the Ptolemies came to power, the Pyramids were already ancient wonders built by pharaohs of the distant past. King Khufu commissioned the building of the first of the three largest pyramids during his reign (2609 BCE–2584 BCE). He chose a location on the Giza plateau near Memphis, which was the capital at that time. Builders used the constellation of the Great Bear (Ursa Major) to calculate true north. King Khufu himself oriented the position of the ramp and directed where to set the first stone.

Writings inside the walls of King Una's tomb date from between 2375 BCE and 2184 BCE. They have come to be known as the Pyramid Texts. They map the route through the underworld that the deceased god-king would travel. They explain that the pyramid provided a way "to reach the heights . . . [as] stairs to the sky, which are laid down for the king, that he may ascend thereon to the heavens."

This modern-day photograph shows the Sphinx poised in front of the Great Pyramid of Khafre on the Giza plateau.

King Khufu's son supervised the building of the Great Sphinx. It guards the Pyramids on the Giza plateau. The immense statue, which has the body of lion and the head of a man, faces east so that it catches the first light of dawn.

This painting by Henri Pierre Picou (1824–1895) shows Cleopatra hosting Caesar aboard her royal barge as they traveled in luxury on the Nile.

For Cleopatra, the voyage with Caesar echoed the river trip she took when she first became queen. She used this trip to stage her comeback and to give her people a chance to experience her grandeur firsthand. The magnificence of her presence left no doubts about her power or her strength as Egypt's ruler. To underscore her authority, it is likely that Cleopatra arranged a stop at Memphis—the former capital where the pharaohs of ages past resided. The priests there could perform the ancient coronation rites to install Cleopatra as pharaoh. Visiting Memphis accompanied by her powerful protector would earn Cleopatra the unconditional respect and loyalty of all Egyptians.

Cleopatra and Caesar's journey also had religious significance for the Egyptians. By now, Cleopatra was expecting Caesar's child. Cleopatra's ties to Isis linked her to the goddess's power over motherhood and love. Isis also had strong connections to water and to the river itself. She was responsible for the annual flooding and for the bounty of the harvest. She protected the fleet and

This photograph from 1894 shows a stretch of the Nile River at the site of Memphis, the ancient capital of Lower Egypt, which was near present-day Cairo.

ensured the success of the sea trade. Traveling with her warrior by her side, Cleopatra conjured up an image of the goddess that left a lasting impression on her subjects.

Historical accounts of the trip suggest that Caesar hoped to trace the Nile to its source. The character of the river and its yearly flood cycle contributed to its mystique. Caesar was keen to discover its secret but, as the story goes, his soldiers insisted that he abandon this quest even before they reached the first waterfall. In fact, the source of the Nile was not found for another 2,000 years.

In May, Caesar left Egypt for Syria. On June 23, Cleopatra gave birth to a son, whom she named Ptolemy Caesar. He was called Caesarion, or Little Caesar.

The Temple of Esneh was decorated with a raised wall sculpture (called a bas-relief, copied in this sketch) of Cleopatra giving birth to Caesar's son, Caesarion, assisted by her handmaidens.

CHAPTER 5

Devotion and Disaster

Do you think it wise at this time to rest on your soft couches and enjoy sweet sleep? Cleopatra has taken over the palace. . . .

—Lucan

In September of 46 BCE, Caesar returned to Rome in triumph to celebrate his victories in Gaul, in Pontus (a kingdom that was located on the southern coast of the Black Sea), in Numidia (part of present-day Algeria and Tunisia), and in Egypt. Cleopatra, along with Ptolemy XIV and Caesarion, traveled to Rome in late summer or early fall. It is possible that they were on hand for the celebration held in Caesar's honor.

According to custom, Caesar exhibited his war **spoils** in a procession of prisoners and treasure that paraded through the streets of Rome. Included were a replica of the

Everyone in the city came out to pay their respects to conquering heroes returning to Rome, as shown in this engraving by Jacques Grasset de Saint-Sauveur and L. F. Labrousse, c. 1796.

Pharos lighthouse, a dummy of Pothinus, and a statue of the god of the Nile. Arsinoë was among the prisoners in chains whom the soldiers marched past the crowd. Last came the conqueror himself, led by forty elephants holding torches to light his way.

Was Cleopatra present to witness her sister's public humiliation? If so, she might have enjoyed the spectacle, given their bitter history of envy and hatred. However, many Romans felt nothing but pity for the Egyptian princess. They pleaded for mercy on Arsinoë's behalf. In a move that must have provoked Cleopatra, Caesar agreed to spare Arsinoë's life. He sent her into exile in Asia Minor.

Caesar's Guest

Caesar arranged for Cleopatra to live in a villa outside the city. It sat amid lush gardens just across the Tiber River from his own residence. Along with her brother, her son, and a team of household servants, Cleopatra settled in for an extended stay as Caesar's guest.

Caesar wanted Cleopatra to feel at home. He smothered her with gifts and luxuries while the Romans looked on with shock and disgust. Life in Rome was simple and modest compared to life in Alexandria. Most Romans did not surround themselves with the costly trappings and plush furnishings the Alexandrians enjoyed. They disapproved of Cleopatra's extravagant tastes.

Apart from their feelings about Alexandria, the Romans thought that women should know their place, and their place was not in the halls of power. Women belonged behind the scenes, not enthroned and in charge. Roman women supported the efforts of their husbands, but their sphere of influence was small. As a rule, they did not otherwise participate in the public **forum**. Romans would have found Cleopatra's thirst for power improper.

Roman Ideals

When the Romans set up their Republic nearly a half-century earlier, they rose up against the Etruscan kings. They got rid of the extravagance favored by the monarchy. They preferred a simple life. To them, a clean-living, hardworking farmer personified the ideal citizen. As a result, they felt suspicious of all things eastern. They associated anything the least bit exotic with soft living. They admired cultural achievements, such as the scholarship of the Greeks and the architecture of the Egyptians. However, they had little respect for monarchies in general, and they disapproved of the Ptolemies in particular.

This mosaic dating from around 200 CE shows Roman farmers hard at work—a quality valued by Roman ideals.

The Romans would also have disapproved of Cleopatra's relationship with Caesar, who already had a wife named Calpurnia. They would have considered it indecent and dishonest to keep Cleopatra and her son housed across the river. They may have blamed the situation on the powers of the Egyptian queen, but Caesar's reputation was tarnished as well.

In this painting by Abel de Pujol (1787–1861), Calpurnia tells her husband, Caesar, of her dream foretelling disaster and begs him not to go to the Senate.

Caesar's Plans

Rumors began to fly. Some said Caesar planned to pass a law so that he could have two wives. He would marry Cleopatra, even though marriage between a Roman and a foreigner was not legal. He would recognize their son as his heir. Some said he planned to declare himself king. Some said he wanted to move the capital to Alexandria. He would make Cleopatra his queen and rule as a god.

Caesar may have considered all of these options, but he did not follow through on them. He did publicly recognize Cleopatra's right to rule Egypt. He renewed the pact established with Ptolemy XII and Ptolemy XIII, declaring Cleopatra to be "a friend and ally" of Rome. Egypt would fall under Rome's protection but would not be annexed to the Republic.

Rumors began to fly. . . . He would make Cleopatra his queen and rule as a god.

Cleopatra must have felt great relief. Her presence in Rome was having the desired effect on Caesar even if it was making his fellow senators tense. It was in her best interests—and the interests of her people—to prolong her visit. Staying close to Caesar ensured that her voice continued to be heard and her needs continued to be met. It also reinforced her claims on behalf of her son as Caesar's heir.

Evidence of Cleopatra's time in Rome may be seen in a temple that was located in Palestrina, a town twenty-four miles east of

Rome. Called the Sanctuary of the Fortune of the First Born, the walls were decorated with a mosaic that depicted the Egyptian landscape along the Nile. Scholars believe that Cleopatra may have paid to have the mosaic installed. She had the money, knowledge, and vision to complete such a project. She might also have felt that the mosaic would introduce her homeland to the Roman people.

The *Nile Mosaic of Palestrina*

The *Nile Mosaic of Palestrina* that depicted the Egyptian landscape along the Nile included the lively city of Alexandria, boats on the river, temples and monuments, and wild animals and exotic plants. In addition, the temple itself honored Isis, the Egyptian goddess who controlled love and childbirth. New mothers traveled to the temple from Rome to give thanks for the health of their newborn babies. Cleopatra may have visited the temple to give thanks for her son, Caesarion. Seeing the temple may have inspired her to give a gift of the mosaic. It would have shown her deep appreciation for, and connection to, the goddess's power.

This detail from the *Nile Mosaic of Palestrina*, photographed by Phillipa Lewis, shows the annual flooding of the Nile, including Egyptian boats, crops, native plants, and architecture.

The Goddess in the Temple

The uneasy response to Caesar's relationship with Cleopatra increased when he completed a building project of his own in the center of Rome. He had promised it to the Roman people before his last campaign. As planned, Caesar constructed an annex to the public square known as the Forum. He called it the Forum Julium in honor of his family.

The addition was intended to help ease the problem of overcrowding in the main square. It featured a spectacular temple dedicated to Venus, the Roman goddess of love. Venus was the patron saint of Caesar's clan, and her statue stood inside the temple. Beside it, Caesar added a golden image of Cleopatra.

Caesar commissioned Cleopatra's statue and displayed it for everyone to see. He let the world know of his devotion to this outsider. Housed in a shrine, the statue implied that Cleopatra was a goddess. This honor extended to Cleopatra and Caesar's son, too.

What's more, Caesar had his own statue added to the Temple of Quirinus, the founder of Rome. Caesar seemed to be borrowing a page from Cleopatra's traditions that blurred the lines between human and divine beings. The senators became more and more alarmed for the future of the Republic.

This present-day photograph shows the ruins of Caesar's Forum in Rome.

What effect was Cleopatra having on Caesar's judgment? The deep dislike and distrust the Romans felt toward Cleopatra only increased when Caesar reformed the Roman calendar to match the Egyptian method of tracking the year. The change from the lunar to the solar calendar caused an uproar. Up to that time, Roman priests decided when extra days would be added to the lunar year. They could delay or speed up events to suit their own ends. They could, in effect, manipulate time. In changing over to the solar calendar, Caesar took away the priests' power. Reducing ways for others to interfere with the political system gave Caesar more control.

As disturbing as the rumors of Cleopatra's influence and Caesar's growing power were to his colleagues, Caesar was still very much admired by the Roman people. His military might was unequaled in the history of Rome. Everything he accomplished on the battlefield benefited the Republic and made it stronger. In

The Julian Calendar

The lunar calendar that the Romans used had 355 days in the year. Every other year, a block of days called an intercalary month had to be added to make the months line up with the seasons. The solar calendar developed by scholars hired by the Ptolemies had 365.25 days in the year. With the help of an Alexandrian astronomer, Caesar established a solar calendar, which he called the Julian calendar. It is nearly identical to the calendar we use today.

This broadside, or poster, of the Julian calendar was created in Germany in 1520.

The scene depicted in this nineteenth-century engraving shows Mark Antony offering Caesar a crown. Caesar refuses to wear it, indicating that he doesn't intend to establish a monarchy in Rome.

February of 44 BCE, the Senate acknowledged Caesar's popularity. It named him dictator for life even though the role of dictator had until then been reserved only for emergencies and only for a limited term.

At this point, Caesar could have claimed sole leadership of Rome without much opposition. However, naming Caesarion as his heir and establishing a monarchy, as Cleopatra might have wished, was out of the question. The Roman people did not want a king.

Deep down, Caesar may not have wanted to be king, either. Much as he loved power, he was more comfortable leading troops than trading barbs with senators. He needed a new campaign that would get him out of Rome, away from the gossip and the ill will. Caesar masterminded a bold and glorious plan to conquer the Parthian Empire (located in present-day Iran). He set the departure date—March 17, 44 BCE—and began making preparations.

Cleopatra, who would be financing the expedition, may have helped with the strategizing, too. As Caesar's **confidante**, she planned to travel with him as far as possible. As Caesar's ally, she aimed to claim her share of the profits for Egypt when the battle was over.

The Ides of March

It was only a matter of time before Caesar's enemies in the Senate took action. They resented the level of individual power he had achieved, and they could no longer tolerate his reckless behavior with the Egyptian queen. Caesar would have to die.

More than sixty men conspired to kill Caesar. They carried out the deed on March 15, 44 BCE—the Ides (middle) of March. Caesar's former friends and colleagues, led by two senators named Brutus and Cassius, stabbed him to death on the steps of the Senate. According to the historical account by Plutarch, "[He] breathed out his soul through his multitude of wounds, for they say he received three and twenty."

Officials read Caesar's will two days after his death. As might have been predicted, it did not recognize Cleopatra. It did not provide for Caesarion, either, as he was also considered a

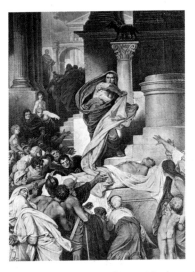

Alexander Zick (1845–1907) painted this scene of Caesar's body on the steps of the Senate as the Romans hear details of his brutal murder masterminded by Brutus and Cassius.

foreigner. Instead, Caesar left his estate to Octavian, his great-nephew whom he renamed as his adopted son. Mark Antony, a brilliant general who served under Caesar, took on Caesar's duties as head of state. He had served as Master of the Horse, Caesar's second in command.

M. ÆMIL. LEPIDUS.
Julius Cæsar.
From a Coin of him in the Hunter Museum

This early nineteenth-century engraving is from a coin showing the profile of Marcus Aemilius Lepidus (c. 90 BCE–13 BCE), one of the three generals who ruled Rome after Caesar's death.

Many assumed that Mark Antony would claim Caesar's power for himself because Octavian lacked experience. However, Octavian soon arrived in Rome to collect his inheritance, which he felt included taking over his uncle's role as leader of the Republic. At the same time, supporters of another Roman statesman named Marcus Lepidus wanted to see their man in power. Marcus Lepidus was already in charge of parts of the Roman Republic in Spain, Gaul, and Africa.

Fleeing Back to Egypt

As the Romans chose sides between Mark Antony, Octavian, and Marcus Lepidus, the Republic was once again plunged into civil war. Cleopatra, now caught in the middle of the conflict without any friends, found herself in extreme danger. Within weeks of Caesar's death, she ran for her life, boarding a ship for Alexandria with Ptolemy XIV and Caesarion.

Many were glad to see Cleopatra return to Egypt. The Roman orator Cicero considered her both rude and offensive. He had been one of her most outspoken critics during her stay in Rome. Writing to his friend Atticus, he said, "The Queen's flight does not distress me at all."

CHAPTER 6

Growing Conspiracies

. . . Judging by her previous associations with Caesar . . . she hoped to conquer Mark Antony even more easily.

—*Plutarch*

Upon returning to Egypt, Cleopatra found herself and her son in a vulnerable position. By then, Ptolemy XIV would have been about fifteen—old enough to demand equal power and old enough to become a rival. Meanwhile, her sister, Arsinoë, was up to her usual tricks, working behind the scenes to sow dissent and confusion. In Cleopatra's absence, Arsinoë had tried to pass off an imposter as Ptolemy XIII, alive and well and claiming his place on the throne. That plan failed, but it would not be surprising for Arsinoë to convince Ptolemy XIV to conspire with her against their sister. Cleopatra needed to get rid of the young king.

Taking Control

Sometime during the summer of 44 BCE, Ptolemy XIV died. Neither the exact date nor cause of his death is known. A document lists him as co-**regent** on July 26, 44 BCE, showing that he did survive the trip from Rome.

Cleopatra once again had Egypt's rule all to herself.

Not long after that, historians assume that Cleopatra either poisoned him herself or had a servant do it for her. In any event, records show that by September Cleopatra had declared Caesarion—renamed Ptolemy XV Caesar—to be her co-regent. Cleopatra once again had Egypt's rule all to herself.

Without Caesar's support, however, Cleopatra faced growing uncertainty. The struggle for power in Rome left Egypt's future hanging in the balance. Would the new leadership change its policy toward Egypt? Could Cleopatra still depend on Rome's aid and protection to help her maintain her own power and authority? Cleopatra had to wait and see.

The Romans Take Sides

With Rome in turmoil and different factions trying to fill the power void, two groups emerged. The **Caesarians** remained loyal to Caesar. Its leaders were Octavian, Mark Antony, and Marcus Lepidus. On November 11, 43 BCE, these three joined forces and formed the Second **Triumvirate** to rule Rome. The **Republicans**— headed by Caesar's assassins, Brutus and Cassius—made up the opposing side. Along with their followers, the Republicans prepared to go to war.

Marcus Lepidus, Mark Antony, and Octavian are shown in this engraving from 1881. They are plotting revenge on the Republicans who killed Caesar.

In 42 BCE, the Caesarians waged two battles against the Republicans in Macedonia. The conflict is now known as the Battle of Philippi. At the battle on October 3, Brutus beat Octavian, but Cassius lost to Mark Antony. Not knowing of Brutus's victory, Cassius committed suicide rather than face capture. When Brutus was defeated on October 23, he retreated into the hills where he, too, committed suicide.

Mark Antony turned his attention to the Roman holdings in the east.

After defeating Brutus and Cassius, the Caesarian generals went their separate ways to oversee parts of the Republic as agreed under the terms of the Triumvirate. Octavian returned to Rome. Marcus Lepidus went to Spain. Mark Antony turned his attention to the Roman holdings in the east.

Mark Antony's Rise to Power

When Octavian, Mark Antony, and Marcus Lepidus set up the Second Triumvirate, Mark Antony was given control of the eastern part of the Roman Republic. This included Macedonia, Greece, and Asia Minor, as well as the kingdoms of Bithynia (part of present-day Turkey), Pontus, Syria, and Cilicia (a kingdom that was located on what is now the southern coast of Turkey). All of these places maintained strong ties to Greek culture and traditions.

Mark Antony had studied public speaking in Athens as a young man and had developed a keen appreciation for the Greek customs practiced throughout the region. He also appreciated being able to take advantage of the region's resources and wealth. The taxes he levied would help him finance future campaigns to expand his territory and increase his power.

Mark Antony (83 BCE–30 BCE)

Besides having military skill and political ambition, Mark Antony was described by Plutarch as having "a very good and noble appearance. His beard was well grown, his forehead large, and his nose aquiline, giving him altogether a bold, masculine look that reminded people of the faces of Hercules in paintings and sculptures." In fact, Mark Antony actually claimed to be a descendent of Hercules. His family traced its lineage from Hercules's son Anton.

Along with being handsome and athletic, Mark Antony was known for his good-natured personality. He was a loyal and generous friend. He could be a decisive and disciplined leader, but there were times when his weaknesses offset his strengths. He never passed up a chance to celebrate with his fellow soldiers and was a fun-loving and rowdy contributor to any party. He could be filled with energy when a situation demanded fast action, but otherwise he had a relaxed attitude that made him carefree and lazy.

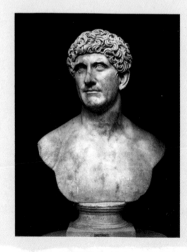

This marble bust of Mark Antony shows the strength and personal charm that made him unique.

In this Roman mosaic, the god Dionysus enjoys a festival with Heracles. Mark Antony was looked upon as "the new Dionysus" because of his love for parties and merrymaking.

Mark Antony toured his newly acquired territories to introduce himself as the ruling authority representing Rome. Everywhere he went, the people greeted him with adoration. His popularity was in part due to his strong physical presence.

All along the way, Mark Antony took the opportunity to collect gifts, tributes, and revenues and happily mixed business with pleasure. Celebrations swirled around him at every stop. Entertainers dressed as mythological creatures played pipes and strings. Admirers hailed Mark Antony as "the new Dionysus," named for the Greek god of wine and foolishness. They looked upon Mark Antony as their kind-hearted patron, bringing joy and goodwill to his subjects.

In 41 BCE, Mark Antony landed in Tarsus, a port city in Cilicia at the mouth of the Cydnus River. The enthusiastic welcome in Tarsus matched others along his route. Mark Antony settled there in order to prepare for his next big conquest.

Request Denied

Mark Antony had his sights set on Parthia—long an archenemy of Rome. Caesar had been planning to invade Parthia at the time of his death, and Mark Antony made Caesar's mission his own. Parthia and Rome had been engaged in a tug of war for decades as provinces along the eastern border of Rome's territory changed hands and shifted loyalties. Mark Antony would need the support from both dependent and independent provinces across the region to launch such an ambitious campaign. Of all the states that fell under the influence of Rome, Mark Antony needed Egypt's resources the most. Egypt would be a key player in his push to the east.

This nineteenth-century wood engraving shows Parthian warriors on the battlefield.

Before Mark Antony could solicit help from Egypt, he needed to ascertain Cleopatra's **allegiance**. Her role in Rome's recent civil strife remained unclear. If she had aided the enemy, she needed to be held accountable. Mark Antony summoned Cleopatra to Tarsus to answer for her conduct.

Cleopatra ignored him.

Mark Antony sent another summons. And another.

Cleopatra would not be bullied. Any contact with Mark Antony would be on her terms. When she at last agreed to a meeting, she harnessed her full powers both as a pharaoh and as a woman to take complete control of the situation.

CHAPTER 7

Passion and Politics

Plato admits four sorts of flattery, but [Cleopatra] had a thousand.

> —Plutarch

While Mark Antony was holding court at the marketplace in Tarsus and awaiting Cleopatra's arrival, word spread that the queen was approaching. As Cleopatra sailed on the Cydnus, Mark Antony's audience deserted him. Everyone rushed to the waterfront to view the magnificent pageantry of the queen's arrival.

Onlookers watched in amazement as Cleopatra's gilded barge approached the harbor with its royal purple sails unfurled. Silver oars propelled the craft, each stroke keeping time to the music of flutes and harps. Cleopatra, dressed as the goddess Isis Pelagia (Queen of the Ocean), reclined on a couch under a canopy made of gold cloth. Young boys dressed as Greek gods stood on either side of the queen, using large fans to keep her cool. Her female crew consisted entirely of maidservants dressed as sea nymphs. A sweet fragrance from the perfumed sails filled the air as the barge pulled into port.

After her dramatic arrival, Cleopatra did not appear in the marketplace as expected. Mark Antony sent word to her, inviting her to join him for dinner. Cleopatra politely refused his offer, preferring not to go ashore. She suggested that Mark Antony and his friends come dine with her on board her vessel instead.

This painting by Lawrence Alma-Tadema (1836–1912) shows Cleopatra aboard her royal barge on her way to meet Mark Antony in Tarsus, 41 BCE.

Four Nights

When Mark Antony and his men boarded the barge that evening, they found a lavish banquet arrayed before them. Twelve tables were set up in the dining room. The place settings and goblets were made of gold and were studded with precious gems. Dazzling tapestries woven with gold and silver threads decorated the hall. Thousands of miniature torches fixed to the ship's rigging splashed starry patterns of light that shimmered on the gilt furnishings and twinkled over the water. Mark Antony could not believe his eyes. He was even more astonished when Cleopatra told him that every luxurious item, chosen especially for his pleasure, was his to keep.

The Banquet of Mark Antony and Cleopatra, painted by Francesco Trevisani between 1705 and 1710, shows Cleopatra about to drop her priceless pearl earring into the goblet of vinegar.

The next night, Mark Anthony hosted a dinner party in Cleopatra's honor, intending to impress the queen with an elegant and beautifully appointed feast. As it turned out, he wound up apologizing for the comparative failure of his effort. He could not hope to match the level of luxury and attention to detail that Cleopatra had so flawlessly achieved. Mark Antony's comical explanation of his shortcomings amused the queen. She responded to his openness and sincerity and his relaxed, easy-going spirit. Mark Antony's boyish charm helped set an informal tone that marked how he and Cleopatra would communicate with each other.

On the third night, Cleopatra once again hosted the evening's festivities. She seized the opportunity to show off her wealth and gain a wider sphere of influence in the eastern provinces. Guests received fantastic dinnerware, delicate tapestries, and magnificent furniture. These generous gifts were a small price to pay for the respect and prestige they could bring the giver. All eyes were on Cleopatra, and she resolved to make the most of it.

On the fourth night, guests waded through rose petals a foot deep as they crossed the deck to feast and frolic in Cleopatra's company. The celebration appealed to many of Mark Antony's weaknesses besides his inability to pass up a good party. Mark Antony loved theatrics. He must have marveled at how Cleopatra could outdo herself night after night. Appreciating the finer things in life, he no doubt enjoyed being surrounded by the degree of extravagance that Cleopatra took for granted. He was also very vain, and

Mark Antony's boyish charm helped set an informal tone that marked how he and Cleopatra would communicate with each other.

being the center of attention on such a grand scale certainly satisfied his huge ego. Mark Antony loved women, and among women, Cleopatra had no equal. She also came to him as a goddess.

The attraction between Mark Antony and Cleopatra was immediate and strong. The queen captured his heart and set fire to his imagination. As pharaoh, Cleopatra had a strong personal and historical connection to the Egyptian gods and goddesses. Forging a union with Cleopatra implied that Mark Antony—already known as the new Dionysus—was divine, too. Together the couple could start a new golden age. Their divine union would inspire all of their subjects, who had closely held ties to Greece. Both Mark Antony and Cleopatra must have realized the

This painting of Mark Antony and Cleopatra, painted by Alexis van Hamme in 1866, shows the couple enjoying Egyptian theater at the palace.

strength of their combined political power as their personal feelings for each other took hold.

Tested Loyalty

Fine wine, delicious food, endless pampering, and growing affection did not completely distract Mark Antony. He and Cleopatra needed to take time to discuss critical affairs of state. Mark Antony had to find out what Cleopatra's role had been in the recent chaos that rocked the Republic. Cleopatra was accused of aiding the Republicans in the conflict between Caesar's assassins and the Caesarians led by Octavian, Mark Antony, and Marcus Lepidus. She was now called upon to explain her actions during the conflict. Which camp had her undivided loyalty?

Cleopatra anticipated this discussion, and she undoubtedly had her version of events eloquently prepared so that she could

Cleopatra's Actions
During the Roman Conflict

As civil war heated up in the Roman Republic, Cleopatra could not afford to align herself with the losing side. Experience had shown that Egypt had to support whoever held the power in Rome.

The Republicans gathered forces in the east with Cassius in the lead. He attacked Dolabella, the Roman governor in charge of Syria. Dolabella turned to Cleopatra for help. Cleopatra dispatched the troops that Caesar had left stationed in Alexandria but did not follow up with any further support or supplies.

Unfortunately, Cassius beat Dolabella and set his sights on Egypt. While Cleopatra waited to see if the Republicans would march on Alexandria, word came to her that Octavian, Lepidus, and Mark Antony had formed the Second Triumvirate and joined forces with the Caesarians. They vowed to stop Cassius and Brutus in their tracks but needed Cleopatra's wealth and resources to do it.

To secure the help of Cleopatra, Octavian formally recognized Ptolemy XV Caesar as Egypt's ruler. In return, Cleopatra promised support to the Caesarians but again only half-heartedly followed through.

Whose side was Cleopatra on? She was on Egypt's side.

give compelling answers to all of Mark Antony's questions. She would convince Mark Antony that she fully supported Rome and respected the authority of the Triumvirate, even though for her, Egypt's best interests always came first.

Cleopatra's Defense

In defending her actions to Mark Antony, Cleopatra expertly explained the risks she had taken, outlined her limitations, and described the threats to her own frontier during the civil war between the Caesarians and the Republicans. She reminded Mark Antony of the long and mutually beneficial relationship the Ptolemies and Rome enjoyed. She persuaded him that there was no reason why this relationship should not continue for the good of all.

In this ancient Egyptian bas-relief, Cleopatra is shown wearing the vulture headdress, representing her rule over Upper Egypt.

As predicted, Cleopatra's overpowering personality, incalculable wealth, and persuasive speech put Mark Antony's fears to rest and captured his heart. Furthermore, he and Cleopatra were forging an alliance of their own. Cleopatra agreed to make her wealth and resources available to Mark Antony in his bid to overtake Parthia. In return, he arranged to have Arsinoë assassinated. For good measure, he also arranged to have Ptolemy XIII's imposter tracked down and assassinated, too.

Cleopatra departed from her stay at Tarsus free of all rivals at long last. She returned to Alexandria to resume her place on the throne and waited for Mark Antony to come to her.

CHAPTER 8

Carefree and Careless

Each day they hosted banquets for one another at which they squandered unbelievable sums.

> —Plutarch

Mark Antony intended to continue his journey and visit the rest of the eastern provinces under his domain. He needed cooperation and commitment from all of the kingdoms in his territory before taking on the Parthian Empire. He spent a short time in Syria, but he could not keep his mind on his work. Within a very short time, Mark Antony joined Cleopatra in Alexandria. He decided to spend the winter of 41 BCE with her. The eastern frontier could wait. Mark Antony needed to be with the woman he loved.

A Life of Fun and Frolic

In Alexandria, Mark Antony and Cleopatra happily picked up where they had left off in Tarsus. Cleopatra spared no expense in providing outstanding hospitality and entertainment. Mark Antony may have been duly impressed at the lavish display Cleopatra had served up to him on board her royal barge, but what he had sampled so far was nothing compared with the rich resources she could offer once he joined her in Egypt.

Mark Antony may have meant to spend at least some of his time planning the Parthian expedition, but he did not get the chance. Instead, he was soon caught up in a daily

"Thou art the armourer of my heart."

ANTONY AND CLEOPATRA.

This illustration from an edition of Shakespeare's *Antony and Cleopatra* shows the lovers in the queen's chamber. In Alexandria, the two of them were inseparable. They found each other's company irresistible.

whirl of outings, parties, and pranks. Cleopatra provided a lifestyle that was tailor-made to suit Mark Antony's cheerful, carefree nature. Mark Antony liked nothing better than to have a good time. Cleopatra did not disappoint him.

When Caesar stayed with Cleopatra in Alexandria, his role had been that of a general in charge of an occupying army. Mark Antony, on the other hand, acted merely as the queen's guest. His troops stayed behind in Syria instead of coming with him. This left him free to wander unescorted through the city, visiting with the Alexandrians as a private citizen. Mark Antony traded his Roman clothes for the Greek style of dress that Alexandrians favored, and he was soon taking full advantage of the wealth and privilege Cleopatra enjoyed.

Extravagant Pleasures

Shortly after Mark Antony's arrival, he and Cleopatra formed a club called "The Order of the Inimitable Life." It was devoted to the pursuit of boundless joy, complete freedom, and endless pleasure. Mark Antony and Cleopatra were its two main members, along with an exclusive, select group of Alexandrians. Their sole purpose was to indulge themselves. They took turns hosting nightly banquets, and the object was to top the effort of the night before. They ate the finest foods. They drank the finest wines. Each evening's fare was more tempting and tantalizing than the last. The festivities were marked by excess and extravagance. When it came to enjoying all the richness that life had to offer, Mark Antony and Cleopatra truly had no equals.

Cleopatra's Royal Kitchen

According to a story recorded by Plutarch, a man named Philotas befriended one of Cleopatra's cooks and took a tour of the royal kitchen. Eight boars roasted on spits, and Philotas remarked on the crowd that must be expected to eat such a feast. "The cook laughed at his simplicity, and told him there were not above twelve to dine, but that every dish was to be served up just roasted to a turn, and if anything was but one minute ill-timed, it was spoiled; 'And,' said he, 'maybe Mark Antony will eat just now, maybe not this hour, maybe he will call for wine, or begin to talk, and will put it off. So that,' he continued, 'it is not one, but many suppers must be had in readiness, as it is impossible to guess at his hour.'"

This painting shows Cleopatra and Mark Antony feasting with a select group of Alexandrians, as was their nightly habit.

During the day, Cleopatra arranged all kinds of activities and diversions meant to keep Mark Antony amused, and she never left his side for a moment. She joined him for lectures, celebrations, athletic events, hunting parties, gambling, and gaming. She watched while he participated in sword-fighting demonstrations and contests. Together they toured monuments and visited sanctuaries. Whatever Mark Antony wished to pursue at any given moment, Cleopatra gladly provided.

Carrying herself with the dignity of a queen did not prevent Cleopatra from staging tricks and playing practical jokes. For example, after a night of drinking, she and Mark Antony often dressed as beggars. They would then run through the dark streets of Alexandria, banging on windows and knocking on doors to wake up the sleepy citizens. They would join other groups of merrymakers partying in the streets. Cleopatra would cheer for Mark Antony as he scuffled good-naturedly with rowdy toughs. Alexandrians easily recognized their queen and her jovial companion. They went out of their way to make sure that Mark Antony was not seriously hurt during these nighttime antics.

Contempt from Rome

To outsiders—especially Romans—it seemed likely that Cleopatra manipulated Mark Antony in order to keep him under her closely supervised control. Mark Antony's behavior in Alexandria stirred up Rome's long-standing contempt for Cleopatra and her exotic ways. The soft, pleasure-seeking lifestyle favored by the people of the east inspired widespread distrust and scorn. Moreover, it was no secret that Cleopatra had ruthless cunning and superior intelligence. Rumors circulated about Mark Antony's inability to think for himself thanks to Cleopatra's power over him.

> *Mark Antony's behavior in Alexandria stirred up Rome's long-standing contempt for Cleopatra and her exotic ways.*

Cleopatra's hold on Mark Antony may indeed have been very powerful. Nevertheless, there is evidence that she encouraged Mark Antony's military ambition and never lost sight of his political strength and his ultimate goals. According to Plutarch, having played a good-natured joke on Mark Antony by exposing his feeble attempt to dupe her on a fishing trip, Cleopatra said, "Leave . . . the fishing-rod, general, to us poor sovereigns of Pharos and Canopus; your game is cities, provinces, and kingdoms." This noble remark shows the faith she put in Mark Antony's leadership and might.

SHAKESPEARE

ANTONY & CLEOPATRA.

This engraving is an illustration from an edition of Shakespeare's *Antony and Cleopatra*. It shows Cleopatra greeting her warrior as an equal—and with hope for their future together.

As it turned out, Mark Antony needed all the encouragement Cleopatra could give him. Boasting and swaggering, he vowed to conquer vast empires. However, when it came to leaving the queen's comfortable palace and blissful company, he dragged his feet. At last, in the spring of 40 BCE, Mark Antony's neglect put Rome's eastern territory in danger. Parthia was on the march. Mark Antony needed to take action. With great reluctance, he hastily left Egypt and made his way to Syria.

CHAPTER 9

Republican Unrest

Cleopatra should have paid Fulvia tuition for
schooling Mark Antony to obey a woman.
　　　　　—Plutarch

The Parthians were not about to wait for Mark Antony to challenge them. Over the winter, they rallied their forces and launched their attack. By the time Mark Antony caught up with them, they had crossed the frontier into Syria and had overtaken much of Asia Minor and Judea (modern-day Israel and Jordan).

When Mark Antony landed at the city of Tyre on the Mediterranean coast, reports from the battlefield revealed a bad situation. Republican troops that fought with Cassius had joined forces with the Parthians; so had many of the local kings who were once friendly to Mark Antony's cause.

Mark Antony's troops that had been camped in Syria lacked organization and leadership. Any effort they made

The Parthians were fierce warriors who were not afraid to take the offensive, as shown in this engraving from the nineteenth century.

to defend the territory was clumsy, at best, and hopeless, at worst. They could not fend off the Parthian attack. As the Parthians reclaimed old territory, many of Mark Antony's troops switched their loyalty to the stronger side. The Parthians were threatening to take over the entire eastern territory, kingdom by kingdom.

The Meddling Wife

The bad news coming from the Syrian front was nothing compared with the alarming reports coming from Athens and Rome. In Tyre, Mark Antony received a letter from his wife, Fulvia. She explained that in his absence, she and his brother had launched a revolt against Octavian, a conflict that could destroy Mark Antony's position in Rome. As critical as the situation was in Syria, Mark Antony had to deal with Rome first. He quickly traveled to Athens to confront Fulvia and find out what damage she had done.

Once he arrived in Athens, Mark Antony found out how it happened that his inflexible and overbearing wife, Fulvia, had started a war on his behalf:

In Rome, Octavian had decided to recognize the service of veterans who had helped to defeat the Republicans by giving them land. Landowners and farmers whose property was being seized for this purpose objected. They did not feel they should lose their livelihood to reward the troops, and they were angry.

Fulvia and Mark Antony's brother, Lucius Antonius, took sides against Octavian, but their complaint had nothing to do with whether or not Octavian's policy was fair. They objected

Lucius Antonius, shown on this Roman coin, was Mark Antony's younger brother. He shared Mark Antony's love of parties, women, and pranks. The date and details of his death are unknown.

Fulvia (77 BCE–40 BCE)

Like other Romans of the day, Mark Antony had female friends and companions far and wide as well as a wife at home. Most general's wives took care of the household and the children while their husband spent months, or even years, on the battlefield. Mark Antony's wife, Fulvia, was not like most general's wives. In her union with Mark Antony, Fulvia refused to sit on the sidelines. She found ways to scheme, manage, and manipulate Mark Antony's career to satisfy her own ambition. According to Plutarch, "Fulvia had no interest in women's work such as spinning or housekeeping and did not wish to preside over a husband who was not a public figure. Rather, she wanted to rule a ruler or command a general."

According to Cicero, Fulvia, depicted on this Roman coin, was Mark Antony's third wife. He divorced Antonia, with whom he had a daughter, to marry Fulvia. They had two sons together.

because Mark Antony's soldiers were not given an equal share, and they wanted to generate hostility toward Octavian. Landowners and their sympathizers were glad to have Lucius and Fulvia involved, regardless of what their motives might be. Such influential support was all it took to generate dissension. Veterans who felt cheated joined the rebel forces against Octavian, and as opposition to Octavian grew, fighting broke out across Italy.

Octavian retreated to central Italy to command his troops. Lucius and Fulvia headed for Gaul to organize some of Mark Antony's soldiers stationed there. When they could not pass through the region that Octavian occupied, they were forced into the hills. Octavian attacked the walled city where they hid and would have starved them out if they had not surrendered. Octavian spared their lives, and Fulvia fled to Athens.

Mark Antony came to Fulvia in a rage. This time, her reckless meddling could cost him everything. The pair had a heated encounter, and then Mark Antony left to try to save his position in the Triumvirate. Fulvia, already ill, died a short time later without seeing her husband again. At about that same time, Cleopatra gave birth to twins whom she named Alexander Helios and Cleopatra Selene—the Sun and the Moon.

Bargaining with Octavian

As Mark Antony sailed for Italy, Cleopatra had every reason to celebrate. She had long hoped that Mark Antony would cut his ties with Octavian. Maybe Fulvia had done him a favor. From Cleopatra's point of view, only Octavian stood in the way of Ptolemy XV Caesar's destiny as Caesar's heir. Combining resources with Mark Antony would allow Cleopatra to make her son's future secure.

She had long hoped that Mark Antony would cut his ties with Octavian.

It was only a matter of time before Egypt and Rome together would rule the world. Not only that, Fulvia was dead! Mark Antony was free to marry Cleopatra. The queen believed that kinship would strengthen their bond and ensure Mark Antony's devotion to her cause. Cleopatra saw the future unfolding before her, a thrilling legacy of power. She would restore the Ptolemaic Empire to its former glory. She would take it to new heights.

Mark Antony landed in the southernmost region of Italy with a fleet of troops. Octavian met him there but did not engage in

ATLANTIC OCEAN

ROMAN REPUBLIC
44–31 BCE

GAUL
(REGION OF FRANCE AND BELGIUM)

DALMATIA
MACEDONIA
BLACK SEA

Rome
ITALY
SPAIN
CORSICA
SARDINIA
SICILY
Actium
GREECE
AEGEAN SEA
ASIA MINOR
Ephesus
Antioch
CYPRUS
SYRIA

MEDITERRANEAN SEA

Alexandria

PTOLEMAIC KINGDOM OF EGYPT

AFRICA
(REGION OF LIBYA AND TUNISIA)
CYRENAICA
(REGION OF LIBYA)

NILE R.
RED SEA

Boundary of land ruled by the Second Triumvirate
Area controlled by Mark Antony
Area controlled by Octavian
Area controlled by Marcus Lepidus

0   200 MI
0   300 KM

This map shows how the Roman Republic was divided between Mark Antony, Octavian, and Marcus Lepidus. Armenia, Media, and the Parthian Empire are in the region east of Asia Minor.

battle. Octavian preferred to talk out their differences. Their troops were not anxious to fight their fellow countrymen anyway. Surely, the generals could come to some meeting of the minds. After lengthy discussions about how to redistribute power and land, Octavian and Mark Antony reached a compromise. Mark Antony would govern the east. Octavian would govern the west, including the parts of Gaul that had been under Mark Antony's control. Marcus Lepidus would govern Africa, the smallest share. In October of 40 BCE, the generals renewed their agreement.

Cleopatra must have had mixed feelings about the renewed alliance with Octavian. Nevertheless, she would have been glad that the division of Rome had turned out well for Mark Antony. She no doubt looked forward to his speedy return to Alexandria and began making plans. They could combine forces to settle the

Parthian uprising. Together they could set a course for the future. However, Cleopatra's hopes were about to be crushed.

A Marriage to Seal the Alliance

To seal the accord with Octavian and prove his loyalty to Rome, Mark Antony—who was newly and conveniently single— agreed to marry Octavian's sister, Octavia. The marriage bond that Cleopatra wanted for herself was about to tie Mark Antony to the power of her archrival in Rome.

Mark Antony's marriage to Octavia in 40 BCE gave the people of Rome a reason to celebrate. It marked the end of the power struggles that caused so much civil unrest. Even though it was a political match, it was widely held that if anyone could win Mark Antony's heart, Octavia could.

Octavia possessed all of the qualities Romans looked for in the perfect wife. She was pretty, smart, and had a quiet sense of self-respect. She would support Mark Antony in all he did without trying to control or upstage him. She was nothing like the scheming harpy, Fulvia— and she was nothing like the power-hungry, foreign temptress, Cleopatra.

This image of Octavia (c. 50 BCE) evokes the essence of the ideal Roman woman. She was said to be modest, patient, quiet, and obedient—everything that Cleopatra was not.

CHAPTER 10

Reunion and Renewal

Does my love not have a hold on you . . . ?
  —Virgil

In the summer of 39 BCE, Octavia gave birth to a daughter. Mark Antony, ready to redirect his attention to the Parthian campaign, moved his family to Athens to set up his headquarters. From there, he sent his most trusted general ahead to lead the first strike. Mark Antony's troops soundly defeated the Republican general who had been connected to Cassius. Furthermore, the battle on June 9, 38 BCE, marked the first time Rome had ever claimed victory over the Parthians

Meanwhile, Octavia and Mark Antony settled into life among the Athenians, who made them feel right at home. Soon the citizens included them in all aspects of civic life. Mark Antony directed athletic events held in his honor. The couple participated in sacred ceremonies, dressing and acting as the new Dionysus and Athena, the patron goddess of the city.

In Cleopatra's time, the city of Athens was a close second to Alexandria in splendor and grandeur, as depicted in this engraving of the marketplace.

They hosted banquets. They attended festivals. Coins minted in the city at the time showed Mark Antony and Octavia on one side and symbols of religious rites on the other. Life in Athens was off to a promising start.

Keeping Peace in the Family

Octavia also managed to keep the peace between her brother and her husband as their arguments heated up and their disagreements escalated. Late in 38 BCE, Octavian called a meeting and insisted that Mark Antony attend. It could not have been a more inconvenient time for Mark Antony to drop everything and arrange to go to Italy. The Parthian campaign was in full force, and there were plenty of things to take care of at home. Even so, Mark Antony managed to get to Italy as directed. He must have been furious when Octavian never showed up.

Octavia also managed to keep the peace between her brother and her husband . . .

Pressing business turned Octavian's attention elsewhere. It seemed, he did not need to meet with Mark Antony after all.

In 37 BCE, Mark Antony again traveled to Italy to meet with Octavian. Thanks to Octavia's efforts, her husband and brother put aside any hard feelings. The two generals were then able to draw up a treaty. Together with Marcus Lepidus, they renewed the terms of the Second Triumvirate for another five years. They also agreed upon a troop exchange. Octavian would receive 120 of Mark Antony's ships to add to his fleet. In return, he would send Mark Antony 20,000 troops to continue the Parthian expedition.

In the fall, Mark Antony and Octavia left Italy. Octavia was expecting their second child. She traveled as far as Corfu (an island in the Ionian Sea) but then turned back to Rome, perhaps at Mark Antony's request. Mark Antony continued on to Syria and set up camp in the coastal city of Antioch (near the border of present-day Turkey and Syria). From there, he could more easily monitor events in the east as they took shape. He could oversee the reorganization of his allies. He could also prepare for his massive expedition. He scheduled the invasion of Parthia to begin in the spring of 36 BCE.

Reunited

Once he reached Antioch, Mark Antony's first order of business was to send for Cleopatra, and this time, she readily complied. It had been more than three years since their last meeting, but time had not cooled their passion. It still burned as brightly as ever. Reunited at last, they spent the winter of 37–36 BCE in Antioch recapturing the spirit of their time together in Alexandria. As before, Cleopatra provided the extravagance, luxury, and excitement that Mark Antony adored.

It is possible that in spite of Octavia's generous and gentle spirit, Mark Antony had never stopped thinking about Cleopatra. His desire for her may have been growing ever since they parted. Aside from his personal feelings, it is likely that Mark Antony realized he could never hope to carry out his Parthian campaign strategy without Egypt as his ally.

Cleopatra and Mark Antony renewed their devotion as soon as they were reunited in Antioch. This illustration of a tender moment is from a nineteenth-century edition of Shakespeare.

Factions and splinter groups had for years prevented Rome from taming the eastern territories. Cleopatra was a key player in Mark Antony's master plan for finally gaining total control. Her wealth, power, and ambition were the fuel that would propel him forward. Mark Antony clearly could no longer live without her.

Two Wives

Cleopatra was only too glad to resume her romantic alliance with Mark Antony and to form a political alliance as well. However, she did not return to his side without plans of her own. Mark Antony needed to agree to certain conditions and meet certain demands if he expected to have her full cooperation. One of her requirements was marriage. The other was land.

Although he already had a wife in Rome, Mark Antony married Cleopatra in an Egyptian ceremony that overlooked his marriage to Octavia. Cleopatra must have felt great joy knowing that her dreams for the future were finally within reach. Together she and Mark Antony would work toward a common goal to fulfill their common destiny.

The news of Mark Antony and Cleopatra's wedding shocked the Romans. It did not take much to churn up old feelings of hatred and mistrust against Cleopatra. She had been despised as an underhanded and conniving witch since her days with Caesar. That her latest scheme involved yet another noble general did not sit well with his fellow citizens.

Although he already had a wife in Rome, Mark Antony married Cleopatra in an Egyptian ceremony . . .

Public sympathy sided with the patient and true Octavia, Mark Antony's wronged wife. Octavia declined to comment, but her brother let his voice be heard. Octavian called Mark

This sculpture of Octavian depicts him as a hero. In fact, he was known to be a weak, unpleasant, mean-spirited man who had trouble hanging onto support in Rome.

Antony's behavior disgusting and outrageous. What's more, **bigamy** could now be added to Mark Antony's many shortcomings.

Secretly, Octavian probably welcomed this negative publicity aimed at his rival. It could only prove helpful in the long run. Rome's destiny was to be ruled by only one man. When the Triumvirate fell apart, Octavian would be ready to take control. He knew that it was only a matter of time.

Cleopatra knew it, too, but she had other ideas about who would ultimately rule Rome. Meanwhile, she had bigger concerns than Octavian's petty remarks or Rome's contempt. She was helping Mark Antony develop a strategy for governing the east. It promised to restore her lost provinces and ceded territories. She had her work cut out for her.

Learning from Past Mistakes

In the past, Rome had appointed its own generals and representatives to rule newly acquired territories. However, once installed, these leaders were never able to establish control. Inevitably, eastern customs and cultures clashed with western authorities. Cooperation and communication broke down, and civil unrest caused fragile peacekeeping to crumble.

Mark Antony realized that once he reclaimed the regions that the Parthians had seized, he needed to find a way to hold onto them. He decided to seek the help of the local kings in order to avoid past mistakes. Granting them authority over newly defined regions would help in two ways. First, it would put familiar leaders in charge of established populations. Second, it would ensure some measure of gratitude. Mark Antony could expect these kings to be loyal to him as the presiding ruler.

The Empire Restored

In dividing the region, Mark Antony gave Cleopatra parts of Syria and Cilicia along with Ituraea (northeastern Palestine), the kingdom of Chalcis (northern Judea), and part of Crete. He also let her keep Cyprus and included several thriving port cities and most of Judea's coastline.

All of this was territory that the Ptolemies had controlled when they first came to power. Cleopatra could not help but be pleased, but she was not satisfied. She felt that the entire kingdom of Judea should be hers so that the Ptolemaic Empire would be complete once again. However, there was one obstacle—King Herod, the ruler of Judea. In order to expand her borders, she wanted Mark Antony to get rid of him.

She felt that the entire kingdom of Judea should be hers so that the Ptolemaic Empire would be complete once again.

Mark Antony declined. He had recently lobbied the Roman Senate to put Herod on the throne of Judea. Herod would soon be in a position to help Mark Antony's cause, and Antony needed to be able to count on him when the time came. In addition, Rome approved of keeping Judea independent. Judea served as a buffer between Egypt and

Herod the Great (73 BCE–4CE)

Herod the Great ruled the Jewish kingdom of Judea. His intelligence, good looks, and charisma made him a favorite in Rome. Left alone to rule as he saw fit, he turned Jerusalem into one of the splendors of the Mediterranean. King Herod's family, like the Ptolemies, had strong ties to the Greek influence throughout the region. As a ruler, Herod proved to be more like the Greeks than the Romans, sparing no expense in surrounding himself with luxury and style. Like the Ptolemies, he could also be shrewd, cunning, and deadly when it came to getting his way.

Great King Herod, depicted in this painting by James Tissot (c. 1886–1894), was the powerful leader of the Jewish kingdom of Judea though he himself was not a Jew.

Syria. It divided Cleopatra's lands and prevented her from gaining authority over the entire region. As a peace offering, Mark Antony transferred several of King Herod's cities in Judea to Cleopatra's control. For the moment, Cleopatra had to be satisfied.

Cleopatra knew that re-establishing the Ptolemaic Empire did not necessarily mean she could now sit back and relax. Her holdings represented great wealth, both in revenue and in resources. However they were only as secure as Mark Antony's position in Rome and her favor with him. Her future depended both on Mark Antony's success and his devotion. She had to do all within her power to support him.

Building an Army and Navy

In restoring Cleopatra's lands, Mark Antony was as practical as he was generous. Mark Antony had traded ships for men and needed to rebuild his fleet. He did not want to leave for Parthia without a strong naval force in place to patrol and protect the eastern Mediterranean coast. If Octavian decided to make a grab for sole power over Rome, he would launch an attack by sea.

Egypt had a fine fleet and an able navy, but Egypt did not have timber for shipbuilding. Mark Antony made sure that Cleopatra received the most heavily forested parts of the region. The extensive cedar, cypress, and oak groves now belonging to her would provide the raw materials that Mark Antony required.

Early in 36 BCE, Mark Antony sent an advance force into Armenia to conquer the region. This would establish a means of access for the assault on Parthia. His plan was to cross Armenia and overtake Media (present-day northwestern Iran). Once he gained control there, he could continue on, advancing on the Parthians from the rear and outflanking them. With Cleopatra's help and the support of the allies, Mark Antony raised an army of more than 100,000 men. The time was right to strike. Internal strife in Parthia had its leaders distracted and its allies defecting. Mark Antony was on the march in the footsteps of Alexander.

CHAPTER 11

The Parthian Campaign

Cleopatra perceived that Octavia was advancing on her . . .

— *Plutarch*

In May of 36 BCE, Mark Antony and Cleopatra left Antioch. Mark Antony headed for Armenia. Cleopatra headed for home. She spent the rest of the year with her children in Alexandria. In the fall, she gave birth to a son whom she named Ptolemy Philadelphus. She must have waited for news of Mark Antony's glorious victory with great anticipation. Success meant unlimited strength and security for the future. In her dreams, Cleopatra could imagine the ironclad grip she and Mark Antony would have on the eastern world. Soon they would use it to destroy Octavian and bring Rome to its knees.

A Failed Expedition

When news from Parthia at last reached Cleopatra, it was not good. Mark Antony's Parthian expedition proved to be a disaster. Incomplete planning, poor judgment, bad luck, and worse weather conspired against him.

Critics said that Mark Antony's failure stemmed from having waited too long to get started or from leaving the fight too early. Both arguments set the blame squarely on Cleopatra's shoulders. Was he slow to leave her side in Antioch? Did he give up too soon so that he could return to her in Alexandria? Either way, many people felt that

The Expedition

After leading his troops across Arabia to conquer Armenia, Mark Antony divided his forces and moved against Media. While Mark Antony pushed on, the Armenian king turned against the occupying army of Romans and massacred them. In October, Mark Antony finally gave up his attempt to capture Media's capital city. His exhausted troops were caught in the snow during their retreat through the mountains. Those who did not die from their wounds or from the arrows of the Parthian archers suffered from hunger and disease and frostbite. Mark Antony's bravery and beloved personality kept his troops going through a twenty-seven-day ordeal until at last they reached safety on the Mediterranean coast. In all, Mark Antony lost more than 32,000 men; some historians put his losses at more than 60,000.

Cleopatra's spell over Mark Antony clouded his ability to make sound decisions.

A Cry for Help

In the winter, Mark Antony contacted Cleopatra from White Village, a fishing port on the Mediterranean coast. He needed supplies. He needed reinforcements. He needed money. He needed Cleopatra's help. He asked that she come to him as quickly as possible.

Whether Cleopatra went to Mark Antony as soon as she could is open to debate. Some historians believe that misgivings caused her to delay. Perhaps she spent time reconsidering her options before responding to his message. Others suggest that gathering resources for Mark Antony simply took time. Mark Antony needed money to pay his men. He would have expected to claim it from the Parthians once he conquered them. Without the spoils of war, money to pay the troops came out of Cleopatra's treasury and his own pocket.

He needed Cleopatra's help. He asked that she come to him as quickly as possible.

In addition, Cleopatra had a newborn baby to care for, and preparing to travel with Ptolemy Philadelphus would certainly have slowed her down. As the weeks dragged on, Mark Antony grew more and more depressed. He took to drinking heavily. He became despondent over his own failings and the loss of his troops. When Cleopatra finally arrived to take Mark Antony and the survivors back to Alexandria, she found the soldiers in rags and Mark Antony in despair.

Desperate Measures

Cleopatra spent the winter of 35 BCE in Alexandria gathering strength. She reasserted herself as the power broker among the leaders of the neighboring states, forging alliances and drawing up agreements. She needed to stabilize her position in order to help support Mark Antony's faltering efforts. Her skills and determination would see them through this setback and get

Cleopatra responded to Mark Antony's defeat with steely resolve. This portrait helps show the queen's ambitious nature. A setback just meant doubling her efforts to achieve her goals.

them back on the road to victory. To get started, she had Mark Antony arrange the marriage of their son Alexander Helios to the daughter of the Armenian king. Such an alliance would create a family connection that would demand loyalty and service.

Still determined to claim Judea for herself, Cleopatra arranged the rescue of King Herod's mother-in-law, Alexandra. Alexandra had failed in an attempt to overthrow her son-in-law. Cleopatra gave Alexandra a safe place to stay in Egypt in return for her help in the future.

In a more positive move, Cleopatra drew up a treaty with the king of Media to combine forces against the Parthian Empire. This agreement enabled Mark Antony to take up arms again and finish what he so disastrously started. In a brief campaign, Mark Antony's troops reclaimed parts of Syria that had fallen into Parthian hands. Maybe the tide was turning. Still, Cleopatra worried, and with good reason. Her efforts to support Mark Antony became more and more critical as Octavian's power grew in the west.

Octavian's Agenda

In September of 36 BCE, while Mark Antony struggled in the snows of the eastern frontier, Octavian was celebrating. He had defeated Pompey's last remaining son in Sicily and had at the same time deposed Marcus Lepidus. The three ruling generals of the Roman Republic were now reduced to two. Instead of gloating over Mark Antony's failure in Media, Octavian praised Mark Antony's efforts and shared the glory, pretending that both of them were victors.

Mark Antony went along with the sham, but it cost him dearly. Octavian pointed out that Mark Antony could now raise armies and reward his veterans with land from his own territories instead of needing to come to Italy. Mark Antony could not very well contradict this statement without admitting that he actually had suffered a crushing defeat.

To stir up more trouble, Octavian arranged for the Senate to host a state banquet. The generals and their families were to be honored at the celebration. Octavia would expect to accompany Mark

. . . while Mark Antony struggled in the snows of the eastern frontier, Octavian was celebrating.

Antony and their children living in Rome. Octavian knew full well that Mark Antony, having announced his marriage to Egypt's queen, would never agree to attend. Mark Antony's absence gave Octavian another chance to remind Rome of Cleopatra's spell.

This engraving, c. 1790, shows a Roman warship like the ones Octavia planned to deliver to Mark Antony.

Finally, having defeated the last of his own enemies, Octavian could afford to be generous. He offered to send Mark Antony part of his fleet and 2,000 troops to help him complete the Parthian campaign. The ships were left over from those that Mark Antony had given to Octavian the year before. The men represented only a fraction of the number Octavian had previously promised to Mark Antony but had never supplied. To complete this hollow gesture, Octavian arranged for the faithful Octavia to deliver this aid to her husband in what could be a joyous reunion. If Mark Antony rejected her, all of Rome would be watching.

Fighting for Mark Antony's Affection

In the spring of 35 BCE, Mark Antony received word that Octavia was on her way to meet him. Equipped with supplies from Octavian, she embarked on a campaign of her own to reclaim her husband. Octavia was ready to forgive Mark Antony any betrayal. She was certain that they could save their marriage and restore their home life. She wanted to win back her husband's affection. With her brother's help, maybe she could.

Would Mark Antony cave in to the sweet charms of his Roman wife? Would he be flattered by Octavia's undying love for him? Would he see that Octavia offered his only chance to make peace with Octavian? Cleopatra could not take any chances. She had to prevent Mark Antony and Octavia's meeting from taking place.

According to reports, Cleopatra reacted with uncharacteristic panic. She made sure that Mark Antony caught her weeping whenever he crossed paths with her. She lost weight, refusing to eat as if wasting away in despair. Her servants confided in Mark Antony, saying that Cleopatra would take her own life if he left her. Her advisers warned him that Octavia was setting a trap and had married him only to further her brother's cause.

It probably did not take much for Mark Antony to determine what was best for him and what course of action he should take. Clearly, his fortunes turned on whatever happened in the east. Life with Octavia meant being second in line to his brother-in-law. Life with Cleopatra meant gaining supreme power that would unite the east and the west under his command.

Octavia was ready to forgive Mark Antony any betrayal.

Whether Mark Antony figured this out on his own or was helped by Cleopatra and her emotional outburst is impossible to say. Either way, when Octavia arrived in Athens, she received a message. Mark Antony told her to send the provisions on to Syria and go back to Rome. He refused to see her, and he would not be seeing her again.

It was just the response Octavian expected.

Octavia returned to Rome, coldly humiliated in the eyes of the world. Even Mark Antony's most faithful supporters criticized his behavior, but Octavia still refused to say anything bad about him. Keeping silent, she continued to live in Mark Antony's home and to raise all of his children from his various marriages. Octavia behaved as an exemplary Roman wife in spite of Mark Antony's appalling conduct. How could he treat her with such cruel and callous contempt? Romans blamed the evil, calculating, eastern temptress, Cleopatra.

Octavian must have been cheering. Anything that dimmed Mark Antony's popularity or clouded his reputation played right into Octavian's hands.

CHAPTER 12

Triumphs, Titles, and Tensions

He decreed that she should have the title Queen of Kings . . .

— Cassius Dio

In the spring of 34 BCE, Mark Antony again set out from Syria on a journey to conquer the east. He launched a campaign against the king of Armenia, who had snubbed the marriage pact between their children. The stakes were small compared with the grand scale expedition Mark Antony had hoped to wage against Parthia. Still, he seized the chance to regain some lost ground.

Cleopatra traveled with Mark Antony as far as the Euphrates River. While he continued on to Armenia, Cleopatra—accompanied by her staff of attendants and servants—went back to Alexandria. On the journey homeward, she toured parts of her empire. She stopped in Damascus and traveled through Ituraea to inspect the territories she held in Judea. She sampled dates from her groves. She took cuttings from her balsam trees near Jericho to plant back in Egypt.

Cleopatra's open hostility toward King Herod and his suspicion of her ensured that the queen received a somewhat frosty reception in Judea. Reports suggest that the king tried to have Cleopatra killed while she was in his company. When the assassination attempt failed, King

The Trees of Jericho

The ancient city of Jericho (now in the West Bank region of Israel) was built on an oasis near the Jordan River. It was known for its beautiful gardens and for the sweet aroma that perfumed its air. The balsam trees that grew there were said to have been a gift to King Solomon from the Queen of Sheba. Resin from these trees was very rare and extremely valuable. It was used to make ointments, perfumes, and oils.

This image of Jericho shows the oasis that would become the site of one of the most beautiful cities in the eastern Mediterranean.

Herod abandoned the idea. Cutthroat turned gentleman, he escorted her safely to the Egyptian border.

A Small Victory

When Mark Antony returned to Alexandria in the fall of 34 BCE, he returned as the victor. He annexed Armenia to Rome. He looted the Armenian treasury. He brought the Armenian king back to Alexandria as a prisoner of war. And according to Roman custom, he staged a triumphant parade in honor of the event. It featured a presentation of the troops and a display of the war spoils, including the Armenian king held in golden chains made especially for the occasion. Mark Antony portrayed himself as the conquering hero even though the campaign was at best a small first-round victory in a prolonged and expanded conflict yet to be waged.

In honor of the occasion, Mark Antony hosted a banquet for all the citizens of the city. The problem was, the city was Alexandria, not Rome. Not only did Mark Antony hold the traditional Roman ceremony on foreign soil, he presented the war spoils to Cleopatra instead of to the people of Rome. Romans who had been loyal to Mark Antony for so long felt angry and cheated, but it was nothing compared with the betrayal to come.

Mark Antony portrayed himself as the conquering hero . . .

The Donations of Alexandria

A few days after his triumphant procession, Mark Antony invited all of Alexandria to join in a public ceremony. Its purpose was to officially recognize Cleopatra and the children by title and to grant them territories. Crowds packed the Great Gymnasium, which was a huge outdoor stadium used for sporting events. Two thrones made of gold stood on the upper level of a towering stage decorated with silver. Four smaller gold thrones lined up in a row on a lower level. With everyone assembled, Mark Antony and Cleopatra sat overlooking the crowd.

Cleopatra, dressed as Isis, wore the jeweled gown of the goddess. Mark Antony, dressed as the god Dionysus-Osiris, wore Greek robes and a crown of ivy. Below them sat Cleopatra's children. Ptolemy XV Caesar was thirteen years old by this time. The twins, Alexander Helios and Cleopatra Selene, were six years

In this nineteenth-century engraving, Cleopatra is dressed as Isis and Mark Antony is dressed as Dionysus-Osiris for the splendid celebration in Alexandria.

old. Ptolemy Philadelphus was two. All of the children wore elaborate costumes representing the various kingdoms of the eastern territories. Alexander Helios wore the native dress of the Median king. It included an embroidered robe and a tall white turban topped with peacock feathers. Ptolemy Philadelphus wore a purple cloak, cap, and boots favored by Macedonian rulers.

Mark Antony opened the ceremony with a speech, likely delivered in Greek. He gave Cleopatra the title Queen of Kings. He then proclaimed Ptolemy XV Caesar to be Julius Caesar's son and named him King of Kings. Mark Antony then gave the two of them power over Egypt, the western and southern portion of Syria, and Cyprus. Alexander Helios, now betrothed to the daughter of the Median king, received Armenia and Media. He would also receive Parthia from the western frontier to India just as soon as Mark Antony gained control of it. Cleopatra Selene was given Cyrenaica (present-day northeastern Libya) to the west of Egypt and part of Crete. Ptolemy Philadelphus received territories in Asia Minor, including the northern part of Syria and Cilicia.

He gave Cleopatra the title Queen of Kings.

From the Egyptians' point of view, the Donations of Alexandria, as they came to be called, did not have any real impact. Except for

Parthia, which Mark Antony had yet to conquer, most of the lands Mark Antony gave to Cleopatra and their children fell under Cleopatra's authority already. Those that were not part of the restored Ptolemaic Empire were not really Mark Antony's to give in the first place. Strictly speaking, it might be said that Cleopatra lost ground, because now her empire was divided between her and her children, and Judea remained out of her reach. However, Cleopatra did not actually give up any of her considerable power. She would continue to oversee all of the territories on behalf of her children, who were still young. It would be years before any of them could assume their responsibilities.

Outrage in Rome

Mark Antony expected the Romans to see that his actions strengthened his master plan for successfully ruling the east on Rome's behalf. He had set things up so that kings would rule the territories according to their own traditions. Rome would supply military forces, collect taxes, exploit resources, and have the deciding vote in any disputes. Peace and prosperity would be the Romans' reward.

Mark Antony sent his plan for governing the east to Rome, hoping that the senate would give its approval. It did not. What's more, Rome refused to recognize

This bas-relief of Caesarion and Cleopatra from the Temple of Hathor shows the respect Caesar's son commanded in Egypt—the respect that Cleopatra wanted for him, but did not get, in Rome.

Mark Antony's marriage to Cleopatra and would not accept Caesarion's birthright as Caesar's son.

Octavian knew that strengthening the east and having access to Egypt's resources made Mark Antony a serious threat. He wanted the Romans to believe that in the Donations of Alexandria Mark Antony had given his vast holdings, present and future, to Egypt—a foreign power—and had not given the Romans anything. It did not matter that all of the eastern territories still fell under Rome's authority and military control; that Mark Antony still governed Greece, Macedonia, and part of Asia Minor; or that maintaining order in the eastern territories increased Rome's wealth and power. Octavian labeled Mark Antony's actions a betrayal.

The Donations of Alexandria hurt Mark Antony's reputation and caused a lot of ill will in Rome. Even so, there were still those in the Senate who supported Mark Antony over Octavian. To keep them on his side, Mark Antony issued a coin in Rome that depicted himself with his eldest son, Antyllus. Antyllus was Mark Antony's son with Fulvia. He was a Roman boy with Roman parents, and by law he stood to inherit his father's estate. Acknowledging Antyllus reassured Mark Antony's critics. They believed that Mark Antony would not support Caesarion's right to rule over that of his own flesh and blood.

> *The Donations of Alexandria hurt Mark Antony's reputation and caused a lot of ill will in Rome.*

Rome Divided

Instead of launching military campaigns to gain territory, Octavian and Mark Antony focused on attacking one another. Each of them hurled insults and barbs in a war of words. Octavian used Mark Antony's actions to keep stirring up trouble. He spread gossip and rumors far and wide. Clearly, Cleopatra intended to rule Rome as its queen. She had brought Caesar to ruin and would do the same to Mark Antony.

Octavian pointed out Mark Antony's faults and failings: Look at the shabby way he had treated Octavia. Look at how he gave away Roman lands that did not even belong to him. Octavian blasted Mark Antony's lack of character: Did he not prance around in the Greek garb of the drunken god, Dionysus? Did he not play at being a king, sitting on a golden throne? During 33 BCE, disagreements and mistrust turned to public accusations and **defamation**. It was only a matter of time before the verbal battles between Octavian and Mark Antony became more deadly. Civil war was coming.

Cleopatra Takes Charge

Mark Antony and Cleopatra traveled to Asia Minor. They spent the winter of 33–32 BCE in the port city of Ephesus on the Aegean Sea. Expecting to engage with Octavian, Mark Antony needed to pull his army and navy together. He called for the recruitment of sixteen legions (80,000–96,000 men). Meanwhile, Cleopatra contributed money and supplies, as well as 200 of the 800 warships that made up the fleet.

Cleopatra was a shrewd, capable, and experienced leader. She insisted on playing a role in the daily management of affairs. Pampered by her many servants, she attended meetings. Flanked by her Roman guards, she consulted with allies and generals and made decisions. Riding on horseback from camp to camp, she evaluated the troops. She collected valuables and packed up artifacts from the region to send back to Alexandria. In other words, Cleopatra performed all of the duties of a queen, of a

This photograph shows some of the ruins of the ancient city of Ephesus, an important trade center on what is now the Turkish coast.

commander, and of a conqueror. Mark Antony may have appreciated her insight and needed her support, but he probably did not like being upstaged by her as he followed her procession through the streets of Ephesus.

If Mark Antony did not feel that his role was compromised by Cleopatra's royal presence, his loyal supporters did. They urged Mark Antony to send Cleopatra back to Egypt. They reasoned that as long as Cleopatra was involved, Octavian would keep using her to turn the Roman citizens against him. When Mark Antony finally did order Cleopatra to go home to Alexandria and wait for him there, she persuaded him to reconsider. She had wealth, might, and skill on her side. She not only convinced Mark Antony that she should stay, she talked him into letting her lead her own fleet.

CHAPTER 13

Gathering Forces

War was declared on Cleopatra, but in fact the declaration was aimed at Mark Antony.

    —Cassius Dio

In April of 32 BCE, Mark Antony and Cleopatra traveled from Ephesus to the island of Samos in the Aegean Sea. Allies there greeted them with festivals and feasting. Princes and kings joined in the celebrations and rituals. Music, theater, parades, and parties marked the couple's stay on

Street musicians like those that added to the festivities in Samos are shown in this Roman mosaic from the first century BCE.

the island. Mark Antony and Cleopatra divided their time between discussing military plans and tactics and enjoying the merrymaking in their honor.

In May, they moved from Samos to Athens for more celebrating while they waited for the army to join them. Cleopatra was well aware of how highly the Greeks regarded Mark Antony and how fondly they remembered Octavia. She managed to win over the citizens with her grace and her glamour. The Athenians gladly received the many gifts she bestowed upon them. To show their acceptance and appreciation, the citizens honored Cleopatra with a statue that depicted her as Isis. They placed it in a sacred temple near the center of the city next to a statue of Mark Antony as the new Dionysus.

Octavian's Fury

While Mark Antony and Cleopatra hosted lavish parties for their allies in Greece, Octavian struggled in Italy. He hiked taxes and cut services to raise funds for the conflict to come. His popularity skidded to an all-time low. Romans endured hardship upon hardship. As his support eroded, Octavian lashed out against Mark Antony and Cleopatra.

In the summer of 32 BCE, Mark Antony formally divorced Octavia. He ordered her out of his house in Rome.

In the summer of 32 BCE, Mark Antony formally divorced Octavia.

Octavian capitalized on Mark Antony's rejection of his respectable Roman wife. According to Octavian, this was ongoing proof of Cleopatra's evil power over Mark Antony.

Further evidence of Cleopatra's hold on Mark Antony came to light when Octavian read what was reported to be a copy of Mark Antony's will. In it, Mark Antony acknowledged Caesarion

A Missed Opportunity

If Mark Antony had invaded Italy in the summer of 32 BCE, Octavian would have suffered a stunning defeat. Instead, Mark Antony declined to take an aggressive position, preferring to defend his territory rather than attack the west. He also refused to break his ties to Cleopatra, as his supporters urged him to do, a move that would have brought many undecided Romans over to his side.

as Julius Caesar's son. He also left large holdings to his children with Cleopatra. However, what was most troubling of all to the Romans, he arranged for Alexandria to be his final resting place. This could only mean that Mark Antony intended to move the capital from Rome to Egypt if the Republic fell into his hands. As predicted, Octavian's charges caused an uproar. Citizens of Rome renewed their hatred toward Cleopatra and their resentment of her influence over Mark Antony.

Creating a Supply Chain

By the fall of 32 BCE, Mark Antony and Cleopatra had moved their base of operation to the coastal city of Patras near the Gulf of Corinth. They set up camps all along the west coast of Greece to create a supply chain heading south. It ran across the Mediterranean Sea to the island of Crete and then on to Cyrenaica in North Africa. This strategy effectively blocked the eastern Mediterranean. It protected the sea-lanes so that

This modern-day photograph shows the ruins of the busy port and commercial center of Patras. Patras was part of the supply chain set up by Mark Antony and Cleopatra.

Mark Antony's supply ships could travel safely between Egypt and Greece.

Having established their defensive line, Mark Antony and Cleopatra sent a majority of their troops north to Actium to extend the chain. Actium was a Roman colony on the Ionian coast. It was located on a narrow strait leading into a bay that was large enough to hold Mark Antony and Cleopatra's fleet. Mark Antony's army set up camp on the south side of the strait.

With their forces assembled and in place, Mark Antony and Cleopatra confidently settled in at Patras for the winter and waited for the war to come to them.

The End of the Triumvirate

At the end of 32 BCE, the pact that had formed the Triumvirate was due to expire. If the agreement was not renewed, Mark Antony would automatically lose his power as head of the eastern part of the Republic without any action or force on Octavian's part. By holding off combat until the five-year agreement ran out, Octavian avoided the stigma of starting a civil war. He had pledged to end civil strife forever, and he did not want to go back on his word.

Octavian did not want to appear to go to war against Mark Antony. When the time was right, he would simply declare war on Egypt, a foreign power and Rome's sworn enemy. Finally, in October of 32 BCE, Octavian felt that the time had come. He announced his intentions by staging a ceremony of his own.

Wearing traditional Roman dress, Octavian went to the Temple of Bellona, the ancient goddess of war. There he dipped a wooden javelin into the blood of a sacrificial animal. Carrying the javelin, he led a procession to the Field of Mars. He hurled the javelin across the field, a symbol of engaging in combat with a foreign enemy. In performing this ceremony, Octavian appeared to declare war on Cleopatra and Cleopatra alone. She had threatened to take control of every Roman—just as she had taken control of Mark Antony. She must be stopped.

Octavian Attacks

In March of 31 BCE, Octavian's fleet attacked one of Mark Antony's outposts. The outpost fell quickly into Octavian's hands, breaking Mark Antony's chain at a critical point and disrupting his communication and supply route. Instead of blocking Octavian's troop ships as planned, Mark Antony's warships sailed to defend supply stations that were under siege. The distraction allowed Octavian's army to go ashore in Greece.

As Mark Antony and Cleopatra made their way north from Patras to Actium, they were not worried. Their plan included fighting Octavian in a land battle if necessary. Mark Antony

Mark Antony thought he could easily conquer Octavian's inferior forces.

thought he could easily conquer Octavian's inferior forces. However, Mark Antony and Cleopatra's outlook soon changed. When they arrived at Actium to set up headquarters at their camp

This woodcut shows a Roman soldier carrying a javelin like the one Octavian threw. A javelin is a long, thin spear with a point at one end.

on the south side of the strait, they found Octavian's army camped on the opposite bank.

Octavian's position on the north side of the strait gave his army full access to supplies coming from Italy. What's more, only a handful of Octavian's ships were needed at the mouth of the strait to keep Mark Antony and Cleopatra's fleet trapped in the bay.

The Standoff

Mark Antony, forced to take action, tried to engage Octavian's forces in battle, but Octavian refused to fight. He had luck, geography, and time on his side. He could simply wait for Mark Antony's supplies to run out.

As the hot summer dragged on, morale and strength began to break down in Mark Antony's camp. Troops suffered from disease and malnutrition. As conditions worsened, allies from neighboring kingdoms left to join Octavian's side. Mark Antony had to do something to break the deadlock. The question was whether to engage Octavian on land or at sea.

Mark Antony's trusted general advised him to march north and challenge Octavian to a major confrontation in Macedonia. This tactic meant that Cleopatra would either have to leave her fleet and travel with Mark Antony or be separated from Mark Antony to lead her fleet by herself.

Cleopatra would not hear of abandoning her ships, and she refused to consider a separation. She may have been inspired by her love for Mark Antony, unwilling to bear being away from him. However, it is just as likely that she lacked confidence in his ability to beat Octavian on land. Cleopatra saw what happened at the Parthian campaign. She could not afford for Mark Antony to lose the battle. If he was defeated, she would lose everything. She would lose Egypt and her legacy, her land, her people, and her way of life. Cleopatra urged Mark Antony to run the **blockade** and break through to freedom. If they could save the fleet, they could retreat and regroup.

Mark Antony agreed.

In preparing for the sea battle, Mark Antony burned all but sixty of Cleopatra's ships. He did not have enough rowers for the fleet, and he did not want to leave the ships behind for Octavian to claim. He then ordered that sails be loaded onto the ships that remained. Normally sails would not be used in a sea battle. Historians suggest that Mark Antony planned for Cleopatra to set sail for safety if she had the chance. Loading the valuables onto Cleopatra's ships also supports this explanation of the events.

The final confrontation was at hand.

This Roman bas-relief shows Roman soldiers on board a warship, ready for battle.

CHAPTER 14

The Battle of Actium

The queen herself was seen summoning the winds,
Unfurling her sails and frantically paying out the
slackened ropes.

—Virgil

The sun streamed out over the calm blue sea around Actium on the morning of September 2, 31 BCE. In order to break through Octavian's blockade, Mark Antony had outfitted his 230 ships with 20,000 infantry and 2,000 archers and slingers. Troops onboard the ships would fight hand-to-hand combat using daggers. The archers would climb the high ships' towers to shoot their arrows; slingers would use leather thongs or catapults to launch huge rocks and flaming missiles onto Octavian's ships. Troops on land stood by to engage Octavian's army once Mark Antony's ships broke through the blockade.

Mark Antony rowed from ship to ship, giving last minute instructions as his fleet got underway. He directed everyone to hold steady once they reached the mouth of the strait. They would take up their position and then wait for Octavian to attack.

Start of the Battle

Once it sailed out of the strait, Mark Antony's fleet held a tight formation facing Octavian's fleet of 400 ships. Hours went by, but Octavian's signal to attack did not come. Early in the afternoon, one of Mark Antony's commanders finally

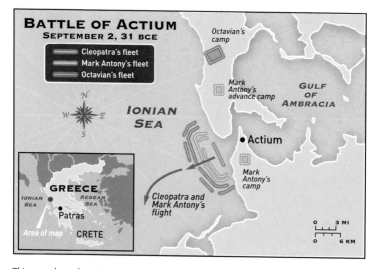

BATTLE OF ACTIUM
SEPTEMBER 2, 31 BCE

- Cleopatra's fleet
- Mark Antony's fleet
- Octavian's fleet

Octavian's camp

Mark Antony's advance camp

GULF OF AMBRACIA

IONIAN SEA

• Actium

Mark Antony's camp

Cleopatra and Mark Antony's flight

GREECE

IONIAN SEA AEGEAN SEA

Patras

Area of map CRETE

0 ___ 3 MI
0 ___ 6 KM

This map shows how Octavian's fleet controlled the coast and blocked the entrance to the Gulf of Ambracia at the Battle of Actium. When the battle began, Cleopatra escaped by leading her fleet through the middle of the blockade. Mark Antony followed soon after.

grew impatient. He moved his ships forward to engage in battle, confident that size and might would enable them to overcome Octavian's smaller ships. In response, Octavian signaled his ships to pull back. He wanted to lure Mark Antony's ships farther out into the open water where they could more easily be surrounded.

The movement of Mark Antony's ships caused confusion in the center of the line. Octavian took advantage of the disorder and commanded the center of his fleet to attack. In no time, a full-scale battle erupted. The fighting continued all afternoon. Each side attacked and retreated and attacked again. Neither side made enough progress to gain the upper hand.

Mark Antony's warships were massive and clumsy. It was not possible to make them respond quickly enough to dodge and turn, neither could they move fast enough to ram into Octavian's

Roman Ships

Warships like the ones in Mark Antony's fleet were called *quinqueremes*, named for the five sets of oars needed to propel them. These impressive ships were big and heavy. A metal covering protected the hull. The ships Octavian used had only two sets of oars. They were small and easier to handle. They were too light to do any damage in a ramming contest— and could easily be sunk—but they were fast enough to get out of the way of the arrows, missiles, and rocks raining down on them from the quinqueremes' towers.

smaller, lighter ships. However, whenever Octavian's ships drew close, Mark Antony's soldiers attacked with poles and battle-axes. They hurled stones and shot arrows from the towers. Octavian did not want to burn Mark Antony's fleet. He hoped to recover Cleopatra's fortune, which he thought might be stashed on board. However, Mark Antony's men would not back down, leaving Octavian no other choice. He called for his soldiers to launch flaming torches to set the ships on fire.

This engraving shows Mark Antony's fleet engaging in battle with Octavian's fleet at the Battle of Actium.

Mark Antony's flight from Actium left his fleet in peril, but his loyal soldiers would not give up. Octavian was forced to set the fleet on fire to claim the victory.

Fleeing from the Enemy

From behind Mark Antony's line, Cleopatra anxiously watched the events unfold. She waited with her fleet of sixty ships standing in formation. When she saw an opportunity to escape, she commanded her fleet to unfurl the sails and make a run for the open sea. Cleopatra's ships raced through the tangle of warships and turned south.

In a move that historians cannot explain, Mark Antony immediately left his command when he saw Cleopatra's fleet break free. He trailed after her along the coast of Greece, with one-quarter of his fleet following behind, leaving his men to protect his interests, defend his claim, and die in battle without him. As the fighting raged on, Octavian proceeded to destroy the rest of Mark Antony's fleet, sinking all but a small number of his

In this nineteenth-century engraving, Cleopatra is shown commanding her fleet and seizing her opportunity to make a run for it.

ships. He then marched on Mark Antony's camp at Actium, overtaking his troops, seizing his equipment, and scattering his allies.

Meanwhile, Mark Antony caught up with Cleopatra and boarded her vessel. According to reports, he did not join the queen in her quarters. Instead, he stayed alone in the bow, brooding for the three days it took them to reach the tip of the Peloponnesus peninsula, the first safe port they could find. During their brief stay, Mark Antony learned the extent of his defeat. He sent word for his troops to retreat to Asia Minor. He would meet them with reinforcements and fight Octavian on land. Cleopatra would sail for home.

Roman historians who later reported on the events at Actium were quick to blame Cleopatra for Mark Antony's loss. Some labeled her a coward. They said that she insisted on a sea battle but obviously had no stomach for war when the conflict began. Others said she was selfish, and that in the face of danger, she acted in her own best interests with no regard for Mark Antony or his men. Cassius Dio said, "True to her nature as a woman and an Egyptian, she turned to flight."

Cleopatra was also held responsible for Mark Antony's desertion. Her reputation as a foreign temptress was well established; using her powers to bring about the general's destruction came as no surprise. Plutarch, attributing Mark

Another Point of View

Despite the blame leveled at Cleopatra, there is plenty of evidence to support the idea that Mark Antony and Cleopatra did the only thing they could do in the face of certain defeat. It is possible that in making their escape they carried out the best plan they could devise once they saw that Octavian had them trapped. If Mark Antony could provide a way for Cleopatra's fleet to break through the blockade, she could get to safety with what was left of their treasury. Mark Antony could meet up with her later, and together they would determine their next move.

Antony's behavior to Cleopatra's spell over him, said, "With that, Mark Antony demonstrated that he was not governed by the reasoning of a commander or of a man or, indeed, by his own reasoning at all."

Cleopatra Prepares for Action

Cleopatra sailed into Alexandria with her head held high. She draped garlands on her ships to evoke a sense of triumph. However, it did not take long to reveal the true nature of her return. To keep order, she tightened her grip on Egypt. She executed opponents caught gloating over the beating she and Mark Antony suffered. She ordered the death of the Armenian king and sent his head as a warning to the Median king, whose loyalty she required. She prepared to fight for her reign.

Mark Antony stopped off in Cyrenaica to begin planning a land battle in Asia Minor. However, news of Actium had traveled quickly across the sea, prompting Mark Antony's commanders to pledge their loyalty to Octavian. The commander in Cyrenaica not only refused to see Mark Antony, but also he executed the soldiers sent to arrange the meeting, as well as any of his own men who objected to his tactics. Mark Antony would have taken his life if his friends had not intervened. He sailed for Alexandria without help and without hope. Discouraged and depressed, he took refuge in a little shack on the island of Pharos.

Meanwhile, Cleopatra desperately tried to secure the future for herself and her children. She started moving her fleet overland to the Red Sea. From there she could cross the Arabian Sea and escape to safety in Asia. The Romans responded by burning her ships just as quickly as she could move them, forcing her to change her plans.

To keep order, she tightened her grip on Egypt.

Cleopatra sent her soldiers to guard strongholds on Egypt's borders, expecting Mark Antony's troops to engage Octavian on land, but Mark Antony no longer had an army. Troops in retreat defected. Troops standing by deserted. Troops facing disaster surrendered. Judea and the other allied kingdoms on the frontier joined forces with Rome. Victory belonged to Octavian. So did the Republic.

Making Final Arrangements

The reunion at the palace between Cleopatra and Mark Antony must have been bittersweet when he finally returned to her. There was nothing for them to do but wait for Octavian's next move. They fell back into their old habits. They renamed their club "We Who Will Die Together" and went back to hosting magnificent banquets every night, vowing to enjoy themselves to the end.

During the day, Cleopatra experimented with poisons. She tested them on prisoners in an effort to discover one that was both quick and painless. She also started construction on her royal tomb, following the Ptolemaic tradition.

It is likely that both Cleopatra and Mark Antony tried to strike a deal with Octavian. In one report, Cleopatra asked that her children be provided for, suggesting that they inherit her kingdom. Mark Antony asked to be allowed to stay in Egypt or move to Athens. Octavian ignored their requests but kept communication lines open. He needed to get control of Cleopatra's wealth to pay his troops in Rome, who were threatening to revolt. He needed to capture Egypt.

Octavian Attacks Egypt

In the spring of 30 BCE, Octavian attacked Egypt by sea on the west and by land on the east. Mark Antony tried and failed to

OCTAVIUS AUGUSTUS.

Octavian, depicted in the illustration above, made his move on Egypt in 30 BCE.

hold off the western advance, losing forty vessels out of what little was left of his fleet. With the help of King Herod of Judea, Octavian's troops captured Pelusium and took control of the Egyptian frontier.

Cleopatra had already sent Caesarion away, securing his safe passage to the Sudan and from there to India. Now she started moving her gold, silver, jewels, and spices into her **mausoleum** for safekeeping, along with a generous supply of wood.

When Octavian learned of Cleopatra's actions, he tried to reassure her. He was afraid she planned to burn her treasury, and he could not let that happen. He told her that he would treat her fairly, though it is not likely that she believed him. Rumors of plots and conspiracies calling for the death of both Cleopatra and Mark Antony had been circulating for months. Cleopatra knew what was at stake and the treachery Octavian would stoop to in order to achieve his goals.

Mark Antony Fights Back

While Cleopatra prepared to go into hiding, Mark Antony pulled himself together to fight. When Octavian's troops moved to the outskirts of Alexandria, Mark Antony launched an assault that temporarily forced the Romans to retreat. The battle earned him a small victory, and Mark Antony returned to Alexandria and to Cleopatra in triumph.

Rumors of plots and conspiracies calling for the death of both Cleopatra and Mark Antony had been circulating for months.

He followed with a frantic series of plans and promises meant to rally his troops and to convince Octavian's troops to join with him. He even challenged Octavian to settle their score one-on-one. Octavian reportedly

Egyptian Afterlife

Ancient Egyptians believed that life on Earth was rewarded by an afterlife, and they looked upon death as a form of rebirth. In order to achieve the afterlife, a person's heart had to be as light as a feather, which came from doing good deeds. Tombs were stocked with necessities to make the afterlife more comfortable, such as food, clothing, jewelry, cosmetics, and tools.

By the Ptolemaic times, most rituals related to preparing for the afterlife were no longer practiced. Cleopatra's mausoleum would have been built as a place of worship for her followers to visit after her death. However, little is known about it. The tomb has never been found, and the royal district of Alexandria, where Cleopatra lived, is hidden below the surface of the Mediterranean Sea.

Tools such as these are among the necessities found in ancient tombs.

replied that if Mark Antony really wanted to kill himself, he should find an easier way to do it.

At the end of July, Mark Antony completed his preparations for a full-scale attack on Octavian. The time had come to take action, and he was ready. He would either defeat Octavian or die trying. Mark Antony marked the occasion by hosting what might be his final banquet, drinking and feasting in the light-hearted, easy-going manner that characterized more carefree days.

An Omen

According to reports, in the early hours of August 1, the unmistakable sound of partygoers, laughing and singing and playing music, could be heard parading through the deserted streets before exiting the city gate closest to Octavian's camp. Fortune-tellers said that it was the god Dionysus, departing from Alexandria and leaving Mark Antony behind.

CHAPTER 15

Death in Alexandria

She mastered the two most powerful Romans of her time, and, because of a third, she was destroyed.
　　—Cassius Dio

On the morning of August 1, 30 BCE, Mark Antony assembled his troops to face Octavian. He commanded the fleet to advance. He ordered his cavalry to arms. The battle was short lived. Mark Antony's navy joined Octavian's fleet and attacked the city. His horsemen immediately deserted. His infantry broke ranks and fled. As Octavian's guards took up their positions at the city gates, Mark Antony retreated. In the meantime, Cleopatra and her trusted servants, Iras and Charmion, made their way to her mausoleum and sealed the door behind them.

Mark Antony's Suicide

When Mark Antony arrived at the palace, news reached him that Cleopatra was dead. Mark Antony could not bear it. He begged his servant, Eros, to kill him. Eros raised his sword, but instead of stabbing Mark Antony, he stabbed himself. Moved by such devotion and such courage, Mark Antony picked up the sword and plunged it into his stomach.

At that moment, Cleopatra's secretary arrived and told Mark Antony that the queen was still alive. Mark Antony had his servants carry him to Cleopatra's mausoleum to say a final good-bye. When they reached it, the door was

This engraving by David Henry Friston, c. 1873, captures Cleopatra's despair as Mark Antony dies.

barred to prevent entry by Octavian or his men. Cleopatra, Iras, and Charmion used ropes to lift Mark Antony through a window. They placed him, weak and bleeding, on a couch. He died in Cleopatra's arms.

Cleopatra was overcome with grief and anguish. She wept over Mark Antony's body, clawing at her skin and tearing her hair. When word reached Octavian that Mark Antony was dead, he feared that Cleopatra would kill herself or burn up her treasury or both. He quickly sent an aide to take Cleopatra prisoner. He wanted to prevent her from doing anything reckless. Cleopatra refused to cooperate. She spoke to the aide only through the closed door, and she would discuss only one thing: her children. She wanted them to rule Egypt. She would not leave the mausoleum without Octavian's guarantee that her request would be honored.

Cleopatra's Capture

The aide had a messenger distract Cleopatra by the door while he climbed a ladder and entered through the same window used to admit Mark Antony. When Cleopatra realized Octavian's aide had broken into the chamber, she tried to stab herself. The aide wrestled the dagger out of her hand and arrested her. He then removed anything that she might use to do herself harm.

To make Cleopatra believe that he intended to show her compassion, Octavian allowed her to bury Mark Antony. Cleopatra returned to her palace to make the necessary preparations for the funeral rites. Within a few days of the funeral, Cleopatra, wretched with sorrow, fell ill from an infection brought on by the injuries she had inflicted on herself. She quit eating, vowing to starve herself to death. Octavian countered by threatening to execute her children if she did not eat. If she wanted to ensure their safety, she needed to meet Octavian's requirements, and Octavian required her to stay alive.

Cleopatra was overcome with grief and anguish.

Octavian came to see Cleopatra at the palace, reportedly at her request. Roman historians who wrote about this meeting portrayed the queen in different ways: Cassius Dio described her as a temptress, using her charms to try to influence Octavian just as she had Caesar and Mark Antony. Plutarch acknowledged her physical and mental condition, depleted by illness, consumed by sadness, and frantic for the safety of her children, if not for herself. He depicted her begging for mercy and offering gifts. In both versions of the encounter, the outcome was the same. Cleopatra convinced Octavian that she was sincere in stating that she wanted to live. He left her with his guards, confident that his prized prisoner would be safe.

Cleopatra kneels before Octavian and pleads for sympathy in this painting by Guercino (1590–1666).

When Cleopatra discovered that the day of Octavian's departure for Rome was approaching, she decided that she must act quickly. Cleopatra had been in Rome for Caesar's triumph. She remembered her sister Arsinoë's shame as she was paraded through the streets. Cleopatra anticipated that she and her children would receive the same humiliating treatment as spoils of war. Octavian could not disappoint the Romans, anxious to see the object of their hatred and the cause of their suffering brought before them in chains.

Sick with sorrow and fear, Cleopatra never considered that Octavian may have had second thoughts about presenting her to the people of Rome. For more than two years, he had been spreading filthy rumors about her evil ways to add to the stories that the Romans already knew. In doing so, he had created a monster. However, the image of Octavian's monster did not match the regal, grieving queen, deeply mourning the loss of her great love—a man toward whom many Romans still felt strong loyalty and affection. Neither did it match the sorrowful mother, desperate to spare the lives of her beloved children. It was possible that seeing Cleopatra might stir feelings of compassion instead of triumph in the hearts of the Romans. Was Octavian willing to take that chance?

Cleopatra's End

On August 12, Cleopatra asked to visit Mark Antony's tomb, a request that Octavian granted. She went to her mausoleum where Mark Antony's body rested and poured a libation, or liquid (usually wine), in his honor. When she completed the ritual, she asked Iras and Charmion to prepare her bath and arrange for a meal to be brought to her. The delicacies and delights the queen ordered included a basket of figs. The guards admired their quality as they inspected the food for vials of poison or concealed weapons. They failed to detect the deadly cargo, coiled sleeping at the bottom of the basket.

She went to her mausoleum where Mark Antony's body rested and poured a libation . . . in his honor.

After dinner, Cleopatra fixed her royal insignia on a letter to Octavian and summoned a messenger to deliver it. When the messenger left, she and her trusted servants retired to her chamber.

Poisonous venom from the bite of an asp was already coursing through the queen's veins when Octavian received the letter. In it, Cleopatra asked that her body be buried next to Mark Antony's.

Octavian immediately dispatched his messengers to the mausoleum, but they arrived too late. They found Cleopatra's lifeless body, dressed in her royal robes, stretched on a golden couch. In her hands, she held the symbols of her reign as Egypt's pharaoh and as the last of the Ptolemaic dynasty. Iras lay dead at her feet. Charmion was reaching with a shaking hand to adjust Cleopatra's crown.

In this painting (c. 1880), the tail of an asp can be seen at the base of the pillar on the right; the viper has just delivered its lethal venom to the queen.

According to Plutarch, one of the guards on the scene rebuked her, saying angrily, "A fine deed, this, Charmion!"

"It is indeed most fine," she answered, "and befitting a queen issued from so many kings."

Then she, too, fell dead.

The long and colorful reign of the Ptolemies came to an end.

Aftermath

After the deaths of Cleopatra and Mark Antony, Octavian changed his name to Augustus Caesar and assumed sole power as emperor. As anticipated, Egypt became part of the newly established Roman Empire. However, fearing the same outcome that had kept Egypt independent for generations, Octavian did not appoint a Roman governor. The assets of Egypt were still too valuable and could turn any ruler into a rival. Octavian administered to Egypt's people and controlled its treasury himself.

Octavian was also disinclined to tolerate "too many Caesars." He arranged for Caesarion to be tricked into returning to Egypt and executed him upon his arrival. Likewise, he slit the throat of Mark Antony's son Antyllus. Ptolemy Philadelphus and the twins traveled to Rome where Octavia took them in, further evidence of her caring and forgiving nature. Cleopatra Selene grew up to become queen of Numidia and Mauretania (now part of Morocco and Algeria). The fate of her brothers is not known.

Finding Cleopatra

Two thousand years later, an air of mystery still swirls around Cleopatra. Was she a selfish, extravagant pleasure seeker? Was she a brutal tyrant who let nothing block her path to power? Was she

Historical Accounts of Cleopatra

A record of Cleopatra's reign written during her lifetime does not exist. There is not a single paragraph giving biographical information, so that even the year of her birth is uncertain. Events in her life must be put together using fragments, artifacts, and historical writings. Many of the references to Cleopatra were written by historians who were her enemies. They had nothing but contempt for her. Many of them lived in the empire made possible only by her death. Most of them were writing about Rome and mentioned Cleopatra only when her actions had an impact on Roman history. If her role had not been so important to Rome in general and Octavian in particular, we would not know anything about her at all.

Egyptian hieroglyphics (writing that uses pictures instead of letters) enclosed in an oblong frame with a line at one end is called a *cartouche* and indicates the name of a ruler. This cartouche spells out Cleopatra's name.

a perceptive advocate for her history and her people with the courage to stand up to Rome? Roman historians, scholars of antiquity, and sketchy accounts support all of these views. The absence of Cleopatra's own voice and only faint words from her subjects leave us free to draw our own conclusions. Nevertheless, on a papyrus dated five years before her death, the queen is referred to as Cleopatra Philopatris, "she who loves her country."

In a small inscription preserved from the final months of Cleopatra's life, her subjects humbly, proudly, and affectionately called her the mother of kings, queen of kings, and kind young goddess.

. . . the queen is referred to as Cleopatra Philopatris, "she who loves her country."

Generations to come will continue to be captivated by Cleopatra's charm. They will be inspired by her spirit. They will explore the complexities of her character. They will examine the evidence of her actions. However, they will never uncover all of her secrets.

In the end, Cleopatra—daring, clever, smart, rich, determined, and rash—wins.

Cleopatra's voice is as silent as the stone used to create this sculpture of the queen during her colorful reign (c. 51–30 BCE).

Glossary

allegiance—a subject's or citizen's loyalty to a ruler or state.

ally—a person, group, or state that is joined with another for help and support.

annex—to take over a territory and incorporate it into another country.

BCE—the abbreviation for Before the Common Era (CE) to describe the years leading up to the year 1 and the start of the Common Era, according to the Gregorian calendar.

bigamy—the act of going through a marriage ceremony while already married to someone else.

blockade—something that prevents people from entering or leaving a place.

bribes—money or other favors given to persuade somebody to do something, especially something illegal, dishonest, or underhanded.

Caesarians—supporters of Julius Caesar.

civil—relating to what happens within the state or between citizens or groups of citizens.

confidante—a person with whom one shares a secret, trusting that it won't be repeated.

defamation—damage to someone's good reputation with false statements.

dynasty—succession of rulers that belong to the same family; a monarchy.

empire—a group of nations, territories, or people ruled by one authority.

forum—a place or meeting in which ideas and views can be exchanged; in ancient Rome it was also a public square.

legion—unit of 5,000–6,000 men in the ancient Roman army.

mausoleum—a large or stately building housing a tomb (a burial chamber).

papyrus—material on which to write, made from the papyrus plant and used by ancient Egyptians, Greeks, and Romans; also, a document written on material made from the papyrus plant.

patrons—people who give money or support, especially to the arts; people believed to be special guardians.

political—relating to the government or public affairs of a country.

Ptolemaic—relating to the Ptolemies and their dynasty in ancient Egypt.

regent—someone who rules on behalf of a king or queen who is not able to rule because of youth, illness, or absence.

Republic—form of government in which elected officials hold the power.

Republicans—supporters of the senators who assassinated Julius Caesar.

resources—natural, economic, political, or military assets belonging to a nation.

spoils—goods stolen or taken by force from people defeated in war.

Triumvirate—three men who were responsible for public administration in ancient Rome (Octavian, Mark Antony, and Marcus Lepidus).

Bibliography

Books

Chauveau, Michel. *Cleopatra: Beyond the Myth.* Translated by David Lorton. Ithaca, N.Y.: Cornell University Press, 2002.

Cline, Eric H. and Jill Rbalcaba. *The Ancient Egyptian World.* New York: Oxford University Press, 2005.

Foreman, Laura. *Cleopatra's Palace: In Search of a Legend.* New York: Discovery Communications/Random House, 1999.

Flamarion, Edith. *Cleopatra: The Life and Death of a Pharaoh.* New York: Harry N. Abrams, Inc., 1997.

Grant, Michael. *Cleopatra.* London: Weidenfeld and Nicolson, 1972.

Jones, Prudence J. *Cleopatra: The Last Pharaoh.* London: Haus Publishing Limited, 2006.

_____. *Cleopatra: A Sourcebook.* Norman, Oklahoma: University of Oklahoma Press, 2006.

Pomeroy, Sarah. *Women in Hellenistic Egypt from Alexander to Cleopatra.* Detroit, Michigan: Wayne State University Press, 1990.

Web Sites

John Dryden's translation of Plutarch: http://classics.mit.edu

Library of Congress site with link to Egypt: http://countrystudies.us

Primary sources, including Caesar, Cassius Dio, Cicero, Lucan, Plutarch, Suetonius, Theocritus, Virgil: http://www.gutenberg.org

http://www.houseofptolemy.org

University of South Florida and The Greek Ministry of Culture: The Actium Project: http://luna.cas.usf.edu

Time line of art history: The Roman Republic: http://www.metmuseum.org

National Gallery of Art: The Quest for Immortality—Treasures of Ancient
Egypt: http://www.nga.gov

Earnest Cary translation of Cassius Dio:
http://penelope.uchicago.edu/Thayer/E/Roman/Texts/Cassius_Dio/
home.html

Bernadotte Perrin translation of Plutarch:
http://penelope.uchicago.edu/Thayer/E/Roman/Texts/Plutarch/Lives/
Antony*.html

Egypt State Information Service: http://www.sis.gov.eg

Ancient World Mapping Center: http://www.unc.edu

Source Notes

The following list identifies the sources of the quoted material found in this book.
The first and last few words of each quotation are cited, followed by the source.
Complete information on each source can be found in the Bibliography.

Abbreviations

AEW—*The Ancient Egyptian World*
BP—Bernadotte Perrin translation of Plutarch; http://penelope.uchicago.edu
BTM—*Cleopatra: Beyond the Myth*
EC—Earnest Cary's translation of Cassius Dio; http://penelope.uchicago.edu
LDP—*Cleopatra: The Life and Death of a Pharaoh*
LP—*Cleopatra: The Last Pharaoh*
JD—John Dryden's translation of Plutarch; http://classics.mit.edu
SB—*Cleopatra: A Sourcebook*

INTRODUCTION: Playing to Win

PAGE 1 *"Whatever Cleopatra dictated . . . man or nature."*: SB p. 103

CHAPTER 1: Birth of a Queen

PAGE 2 *"Egypt has three hundred cities . . . rules them all."*: SB p. 13
PAGE 7 *"the greatest emporium in the inhabited world."*: LDP p. 18

CHAPTER 2: Power and Exile

PAGE 11 *"The Queen, the Lady . . . who loves her father."*: SB p. 37
PAGE 18 *"King Ptolemy . . . father."*: BTM p. 18
PAGE 18 *"a friend and ally"*: BTM p. 18

CHAPTER 3: Appealing to Caesar

PAGE 19 *"Interaction with her was captivating . . ."*: SB p. 32
PAGE 21 *"Whoever has dealings . . . a free man."*: SB p. 40

PAGE 22 *"He is said to have been tall . . . good health."*: SB p. 47
PAGE 23 *"interaction with [Cleopatra] . . . was stimulating."*: SB pp. 32–33

CHAPTER 4: Fighting for Control
PAGE 25 *"Caesar handed over . . . loyalty and protection."*: SB p. 61
PAGE 29 *"to reach the heights . . . the heavens."*: AEW p. 61

CHAPTER 5: Devotion and Disaster
PAGE 32 *"Do you think it wise . . . taken over the palace."*: SB p. 71
PAGE 35 *"a friend and ally"*: BTM p. 29
PAGE 40 *"[He] breathed out his soul . . . three-and-twenty."*: LDP p. 52
PAGE 41 *"The Queen's flight does not distress me at all."*: LDP p.53

CHAPTER 6: Growing Conspiracies
PAGE 42 *"Judging by her previous associations . . . more easily."*: SB pp. 101–102
PAGE 45 *"a very good and noble appearance . . . and sculptures."*: JD p. 3
PAGE 46 *"the new Dionysus,"*: LDP p. 58
PAGE 46 *"the new Dionysus,"*: LDP p. 58

CHAPTER 7: Passion and Politics
PAGE 48 *"Plato admits four sorts of flattery . . . a thousand."*: JD p. 14

CHAPTER 8: Carefree and Careless
PAGE 55 *"Each day they hosted . . . unbelievable sums."*: SB p. 104
PAGE 57 *"The cook laughed . . . at his hour.'"*: JD p. 13
PAGE 59 *"Leave . . . the fishing-rod . . . and kingdoms."*: LP p. 72

CHAPTER 9: Republican Unrest
PAGE 61 *"Cleopatra should have paid . . . obey a woman."*: SB p. 97
PAGE 63 *"Fulvia had no interest . . . command a general."*: LP p.79

CHAPTER 10: Reunion and Renewal
PAGE 67 *"Does my love not have a hold on you . . . ?"*: SB p. 122

CHAPTER 11: The Parthian Campaign
PAGE 75 *"Cleopatra perceived . . . advancing on her."* : SB p. 110

CHAPTER 12: Triumphs, Titles, and Tensions
PAGE 82 *"He decreed . . . the title Queen of Kings."*: SB p. 117

CHAPTER 13: Gathering Forces
PAGE 90 *"War was declared on Cleopatra . . . Mark Antony."*: SB p. 148

CHAPTER 14: The Battle of Actium
PAGE 98 *"The queen herself was . . . slackened ropes."*: SB p. 178
PAGE 102 *"True to her nature . . . turned to flight."*: EC p. 509
PAGE 103 *"With that, Mark Antony . . . reasoning at all."*: SB p.156

CHAPTER 15: Death in Alexandria
PAGE 109 *"She mastered the two . . . she was destroyed."*: SB p.198
PAGE 115 *"A fine deed, this . . . so many kings."*: BP p. 329
PAGE 115 *"too many Caesars."*: SB 187

Image Credits

Classical Numismatic Group, Inc.: 62
© Paul Almasy/Corbis: 17
© The Art Archive/Corbis: 114
© Bettmann/Corbis: 5, 8, 12, 14, 21, 24, 26, 30, 35, 39, 40, 45, 54, 56, 58, 60, 67, 69, 71, 77, 95, 97, 100, 101, 105, 110
© Brooklyn Museum/Corbis: 73
© Burstein Collection/Corbis: 46
© Christie's Images/Corbis: 49
© Araldo de Luca/Corbis: 112
© Fine Art Photographic Library/Corbis: 52
© Historical Picture Archive/Corbis: 7, 83
© Mimmo Jodice/Corbis: 90
© Philippa Lewis/Edifice/Corbis: 36
© Gianni Dagli Orti/Corbis: 4, 107
© Rachel Royse/Corbis: 93
© Stapleton Collection/Corbis: 32, 79
© Summerfield Press/Corbis: 50
© Sandro Vannini/Corbis: 117
© Roger Wood/Corbis: 34
Gabriel Bojorquez/www.flickr.com: 16
Joe Geranio/www.flickr.com: 63
John Havel/www.flickr.com: 29
Ahmet Rasit/www.flickr.com: 89
Hulton Archive/Getty Images: 66
The Granger Collection, New York: 2, 19, 31 (bottom), 38, 41, 43, 47, 61, 85, 102, 116
Library of Congress: 22, 23, 31 (top), 86
Maps by Jim McMahon: 6, 65, 99
Mary Evans Picture Library: 28
Hulton Archive/Getty Images/Newscom: 13
Public domain: 15, 37
Cover art: akg-images/Rabatti-Domingie

About the Author

Susan Blackaby earned a degree in Western Civilization from the University of California at Santa Cruz before moving to Portland, Oregon. Getting reacquainted with Cleopatra allowed her to poke around in the Ancient Greek and Latin cupboard of her brain, sealed up like an Egyptian tomb for decades. Susan has worked in educational publishing for more than twenty-five years and has written dozens of fiction and nonfiction titles, specializing in books for beginning readers. Her first picture book, *Rembrandt's Hat*, was published in 2002.

Index

Achillas, 18, 20, 25, 26
Actium, Battle of
    burning ships preparing for, 97
    destruction of fleet, 101–102
    fleeing from, 101–103
    gathering forces for, 90–97
    map illustrating, 99
    Mark Antony deserting command, 101–102
    Octavian winning, 104
    start of, 98–100
    supply chain for, 92–93
Afterlife, belief in, 107
Alexander Helios, 64, 78, 84–85
Alexander the Great, 2–3, 5, 10
Alexandria
    about, 5–8
    donations of, 84–86
    Julius Caesar in, 21–23, 26–27
    Mark Antony/Cleopatra fun in, 55–59
Alexandrian War, 25–26, 27
Allegiance, 47, 118
Ally, 18, 35, 39, 69, 118
Annex, 27, 118
Antioch, 69, 75
Apollodorus, 23
Archilaus, 12
Armenia, 65, 74, 75, 76, 82, 83–84, 85, 103
Arsinoë, 5, 18, 24, 26, 27, 33, 42, 54
Asp, killing Cleopatra, 114
Athens, Mark Antony in, 44, 62, 67–68, 91
BCE (Before Common Era), 2, 118
Berenice, 5, 11–12
Bigamy, 71, 118
Birth, of Cleopatra, 1
Blockades, 97, 98, 99, 103, 118
Bribes, 10, 12, 26, 118
Brothers, of Cleopatra, 5
Brutus, 40, 43, 44, 53
Buchis bull, 15, 16
Caesarians, 43, 44, 52, 53, 54, 118

Caesarion (Ptolemy XV Caesar), 31, 39, 40–41, 43, 64, 84, 87, 91–92, 106, 115
Capture, of Cleopatra, 111–113
Cassius, 40, 43, 44, 53
Charm, of Cleopatra, 24
Cicero, 41, 63
Civil, defined, 118
Civil war, 19
Cleopatra Selene, 64, 84–85, 115
Cleopatra VII, as historical name, 5, 13
Confidante, 39, 118
Defamation, 88, 118
Dynasty, 2, 118
Early years
    Alexandria and, 5–8
    brothers and sisters, 5
Education, 8–9
Egypt
    belief in afterlife, 107
    Octavian attacking, 105–108
    Ptolemaic empire restored, 72–73
    respect for and from, 14–15
    returning from Rome to, 41
    status with Rome, 35, 43
Empire, 2–3, 118
Exile, Cleopatra in, 12, 18
Forum, 33, 37, 118
Fulvia, 62–63, 66
Gabinius, 12
Glossary, 118–119
Herod, King of Judea, 72–73, 82–83, 106
Ides of March, 40–41
Iras and Charmion, 109, 110, 113, 114–115
Isis, 14, 15, 30–31, 36, 84, 85, 91
Jericho, 82, 83
Julian calendar, 38
Julius Caesar
    in Alexandria, 21–23
    battle with Ptolemy, 25–26
    biographical sketch, 22
    bold conquest plan, 39
    guest of, in Rome, 33–34
    increased power of, 38–39

loving Cleopatra, 23, 28
murder of, 40
Nile cruise with Cleopatra, 28–31
Pompey and, 11, 19–21, 22
relying on, 22–23
return to Rome, 32–33
son with. See Caesarion (Ptolemy XV Caesar)
with two women, 34, 35
Kitchen, of Cleopatra, 57
Legacy, of Cleopatra, 115–117
Legions, 28, 88, 118
Marcus Lepidus, 41, 43, 44, 52, 53, 65, 68, 78
Mark Antony. See also Actium, Battle of
    to Asia Minor, 88–89
    assuming duties as head of state, 41
    attraction to, 51–52
    bargaining with Octavian, 64–66
    biographical sketch, 45
    building army/navy, 74
    defending actions to, 54
    extravagant pleasures with, 57–59
    faith in, 59
    four nights of entertainment with, 49–52
    Fulvia and, 62–63, 66
    fun/frolic with, 55–57, 104–105
    learning from past mistakes, 71–72
    marriage to, 70–71
    meeting in Tarsus, 47, 48
    Octavia and. See Octavia
    Octavian and. See Octavian
    power struggle with, 1, 47, 48, 89
    responding to failure of, 76–78
    reuniting with, 69–70
    rise to power, 44–46
    Roman displeasure with, 59, 86–87
    suicide of, 109–110
    to Syria, 60
    testing loyalty, 52–53
    visiting tomb of, 113

Marriage, of Mark
    Antony/Octavia, 66
Marriage, to brothers, 13, 27
Marriage, to Mark Antony,
    70–71
Mausoleum, 106, 107, 109–
    110, 113–114, 118
Memphis, 29, 30, 31
Nile Mosaic of Palestrina, 36
Nile River
    about, 17
    Buchis bull on, 15
    cruise with Caesar on, 28–
    31
Octavia, 66, 67–68, 70–71,
    79, 80–81, 88, 91, 115
Octavian
    agenda of, 78–80, 81
    attacking Egypt, 105–108
    attacking Mark Antony and
        Cleopatra, 94–96. See also
        Actium, Battle of
    as Augustus Caesar, 115
    bargaining with Mark
        Antony, 64–66
    on bigamy of Mark Antony,
        70–71
    calling Mark Antony to Italy,
        68
    capturing Cleopatra, 111–
        113
    declaring war on Cleopatra,
        94
    fighting with Mark Antony,
        87–88, 92, 106–108
    Fulvia/Lucius Antonius and,
        62–64
    fury of, at Mark Antony and
        Cleopatra, 91–92
    gaining power, 41
    Mark Antony commanders
        going to, 103–104
    seeing threat of Mark
        Antony, 87
    standoff with, 96–97
Papyrus, 18, 118
Parthian Empire/campaign,
    39, 47, 60, 61–62, 65, 67,
    68, 69, 72, 74, 75–79,
    80, 85, 86
Patrons, 8, 118
Pelusium, 19, 20, 21–22, 23,
    25, 106
Pharaoh, word origin, 4

Pharos lighthouse, 6–7
Poisons, experiments with,
    105
Political, 9, 118
Pompey, 11, 13, 19–21, 22
Pothinus, 18, 20, 21–22, 25,
    33
Power
    Berenice rise and fall from,
        11–12
    evil, over Mark Antony, 81,
        91, 113
    family betrayal and, 11–13
    importance of, to Cleopatra,
        1
    marriage to Mark Antony
        and, 71
    return to, 27–28, 42–43
    rise to, 13–14
    taking charge, 88–89
Ptolemaic Empire (dynasty),
    3, 10, 72–73, 86, 107,
    114, 118
Ptolemy Auletes (father), 2, 3,
    12–13
Ptolemy family, 2–5
Ptolemy Philadelphus, 75, 77,
    85, 115
Ptolemy XIII, 5, 13, 16, 18,
    20, 21–23, 24, 26, 35, 42
Ptolemy XIV, 5, 24, 27, 32, 41,
    42
Ptolemy XV Caesar. See
    Caesarion (Ptolemy XV
    Caesar)
Pyramids, 28, 29
Quinqueremes, 100
Regent, 42, 43, 118
Republicans, 43–44, 52, 53,
    54, 119
Republic, defined, 119. See
    also Roman Republic
Resources, 20, 119
Roman conflict
    Cleopatra defending
        actions, 54
    Cleopatra role in, 52–53
    Ides of March and, 40–41
    two sides in, 43–44
Roman ideals, 34
Roman Republic, 9–10
    about, 10
    Caesar, Pompey and, 11,
        19–21, 22

Cleopatra's early rule and,
    16
supporting Ptolemies, 9–10,
    11, 27–28
Roman ships, 100
Rome
    Cleopatra as goddess in, 37
    Cleopatra as guest in, 33–
        34, 35–39
    displeasure with Mark
        Antony, 59, 86–87
    distrust of Cleopatra, 37–38
    Forum in, 37
    Julius Caesar returning to,
        32–33
    returning to Egypt from, 41
Sanctuary of the Fortune of
    the First Born, 36
Sibling treachery, 11–12, 18
Sisters, of Cleopatra, 5
Sphinx, 28, 29
Spoils, 32–33, 84, 112, 119
Suicide, of Cleopatra, 113–
    115
Suicide, of Mark Antony, 109–
    110
Theodotus, 18, 20, 21
Timeline, iv
Triumvirate
    defined, 119
    end of, 71, 94
    Second, 43, 44, 53, 64, 68
Twins, of Cleopatra, 64, 84–
    85, 115